MUSIC LITERATURE

A WORKBOOK FOR ANALYSIS

VOLUME II: POLYPHONY

GORDON HARDY AND ARNOLD FISH

JUILLIARD SCHOOL OF MUSIC

DODD, MEAD & COMPANY   NEW YORK   TORONTO   1972

JACK M. WATSON
Dean, College-Conservatory of Music
of the University of Cincinnati
Advisory Editor to Dodd, Mead & Company

Library of Congress catalog card number: 62-19671

Printed in the United States of America

Third Printing

EDITOR'S INTRODUCTION

Comprehensive and well-rounded musicianship is a trinity of three interrelated and interacting elements—musical technique, musical intuition, and musical intelligence. Musical technique for the performer means skillful and expert control of the media of musical performance; for the composer, it means the craft of musical composition. Musical intuition supplies the creative, imaginative, and emotional dimension of music; it is as essential to the performer as to the composer. Musical intelligence, for performer and composer alike, involves an array of facilities—facility in aural perception and discrimination and in realization of the score; insight into the relations of musical structure, style, and interpretation; understanding of the materials and stylistic elements and determinants of music; and so on.

In this second volume of *Music Literature: A Workbook for Analysis*, Messrs. Hardy and Fish have, as in the first volume, centered squarely on problems central to the development of musical intelligence. The prime difference is in musical subject matter. By focusing analytical attention on polyphonic music, they provide the opportunity for students using the volume to deepen and extend their understanding and insight into the phenomena of music. At the same time, the intuitive and the technical are by no means ignored. Students are encouraged to use some of the works as models for their own creative efforts, and they are advised to play and sing the music and to search out clues for performance and interpretation.

Jack M. Watson

Cincinnati, Ohio

FOREWORD

Volume II of *Music Literature: A Workbook for Analysis* presents a wide sampling of contrapuntal music. The concentration is on the two great eras of common practice, the Renaissance and the Baroque. Many examples of forms and styles from the other periods—the medieval, classic, romantic, and the twentieth century—are offered as well. The works have been carefully tested in our second- and third-year classes in Literature and Materials of Music at Juilliard. The flexible, creative teacher will adapt the material to the specific needs of his own classes.

Some selections will work well as models for the students' written exercises and compositions. Other works can be studied with the focus on formal analysis or comparison of styles. No specific order in dealing with the compositions is prescribed or, for that matter, necessarily desirable. A variety of approaches to analysis is recommended.

Each unit is preceded by a list of Suggestions and Questions for Analysis and Discussion, and in some of the units, as in Volume I (Homophony), sample analyses are provided as a guide to analytical procedures.

Analysis by "eye" only can result in a rather superficial "exam-passing" attitude on the part of students. Only through direct and specific reference to what is *heard* can the whole activity of analysis become meaningful. The authors suggest that each piece be played or sung, using whatever means are available in the class. At all times, the direct relationship between the analysis and the performance of a work should be searched out, discussed, and applied.

G. H.
A. F.

May 1, 1966

The authors gratefully acknowledge the valuable contribution of Deborah Kaufman for translations; Monica Jakuc, Alison Rivers, and Michael Czajkowski for proofreading; and the indispensable aid of Bennett Ludden, chief librarian, and his staff at the Juilliard library.

CONTENTS

UNIT III. POLYPHONY FROM THE SIXTEENTH CENTURY
COUNTERPOINT IN TWO PARTS

UNIT IV. POLYPHONY FROM THE SIXTEENTH CENTURY
COUNTERPOINT IN THREE OR MORE PARTS

UNIT V. *POLYPHONY FROM THE NINTH CENTURY*
TO THE FIFTEENTH CENTURY

UNIT VI. *POLYPHONY FROM THE EIGHTEENTH*
AND NINETEENTH CENTURIES

UNIT VII. *POLYPHONY FROM THE TWENTIETH CENTURY*

APPENDIX

UNIT I

POLYPHONY FROM THE BAROQUE ERA

COUNTERPOINT IN TWO PARTS

SUGGESTIONS AND QUESTIONS FOR ANALYSIS AND DISCUSSION

A. Perform the music.
   (Use whatever means are available to the class: piano, other instruments, or voices.)

B. Determine the basic key of the work.
   Point out the principle elements that define the tonality.

C. Examine the rhythmic structure.
   1. Perform each individual voice by clapping or tapping the rhythm. Comment on the rhythmic patterns.
   2. Perform the combined voices rhythmically. What observations can be made about rhythmic drive? cadences? climaxes?

D. Discuss the relationship between the voices.
   1. Motivic
   2. Rhythmic
   3. Intervalic
   4. Directional

E. Outline the formal structure.
   1. Entries, episodes, etc.
   2. Key relationships. (Identify and compare the cadences.)
   3. Recurring sections
   4. Other features

F. Study the contrapuntal techniques and discuss the use of compositional devices. (Imitation, invertible counterpoint, sequence, etc.)

G. Analyze the harmony.
   1. Using Roman numerals and figured bass symbols, indicate the harmonic function of each chord.
   2. Circle and name the nonharmonic tones.
   3. Locate and explain modulations.

H. Discuss other significant aspects which lead to an intelligent musical performance.
   1. Rhythm and tempo
   2. High points
   3. Change of texture
   4. Stylistic considerations
   5. Text *

I. Compare works of similar form.
   1. Motivic material
   2. Rhythmic figures
   3. Modulations
   4. Compositional devices
   5. Texture

*Translation appears on p. 321.

Bach, *Partita III*, Fantasia
(A) Harmonic study, nonharmonic tones

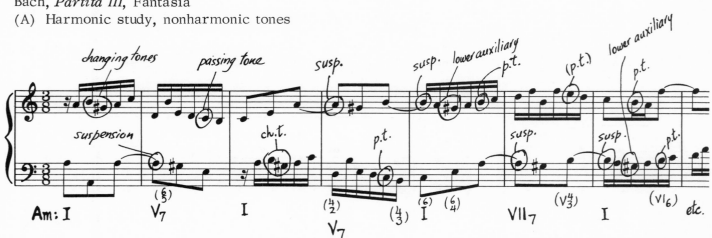

Observations:

1. Imitation begins at the octave in measure 3 in the left hand.

2. Rhythm: 16th-note pattern (Motive 1) alternates between the voices every two measures (continuous 16th-note motion)

3. The third note of Motive 2 (8th-note pattern) ties into a suspension each time.

4. All non-harmonic tones are approached or left by step. The suspensions occur on the strong beat of the measure.

Bach, *Bourrée*
(B) Intervalic study, observations on motive, rhythm, etc.

Observations

(a) Motive outlines tonic triad. Starts on up-beat with leap of a third, descends by step, and ends with leap of a fifth.

(b) Bass imitates the motive at the octave after two beats.

(c) Bass imitates at the fifth below after two beats.

(d) Sequential pattern in both voices.

(e) Beginning material is repeated (with modification).

(f) Rhythmic imitation in bass for three and one-half measures after two beats.

(g) Rhythmic pattern ♩ ♫ appears throughout, but note change at the cadences.

Additional observations:

Phrase I establishes the tonic (A Major)
Phrase II moves to the dominant (E Major)
All dissonant intervals (9ths, 4ths, 7ths) are approached or left by step.

BOURRÉE

from *Overture in F Major*

Bach

MINUET

from *French Suite No. 3*

Bach

ALLEGRO

from *Suite No. 10*

Handel

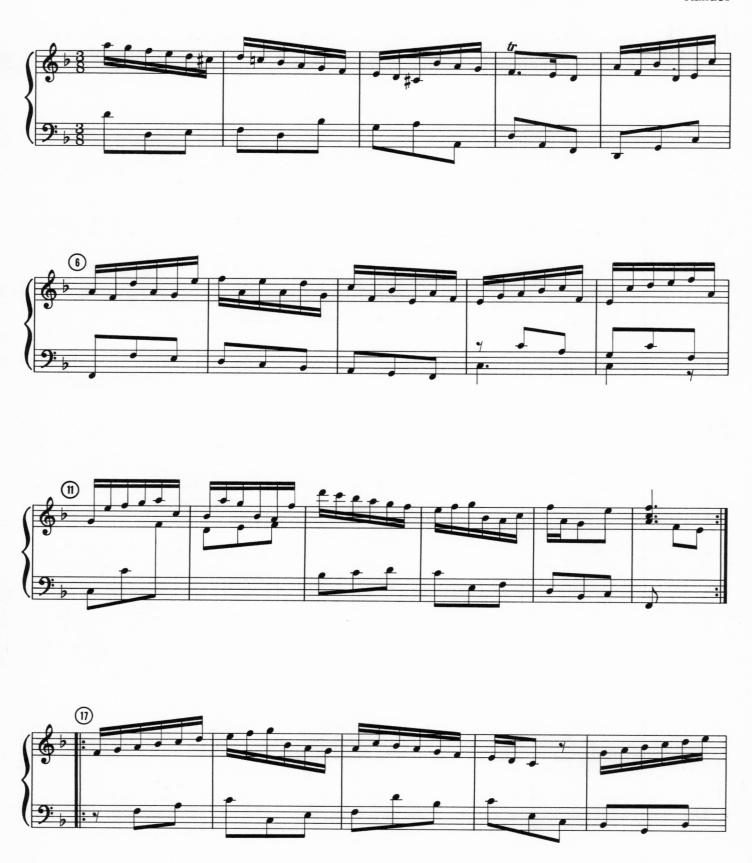

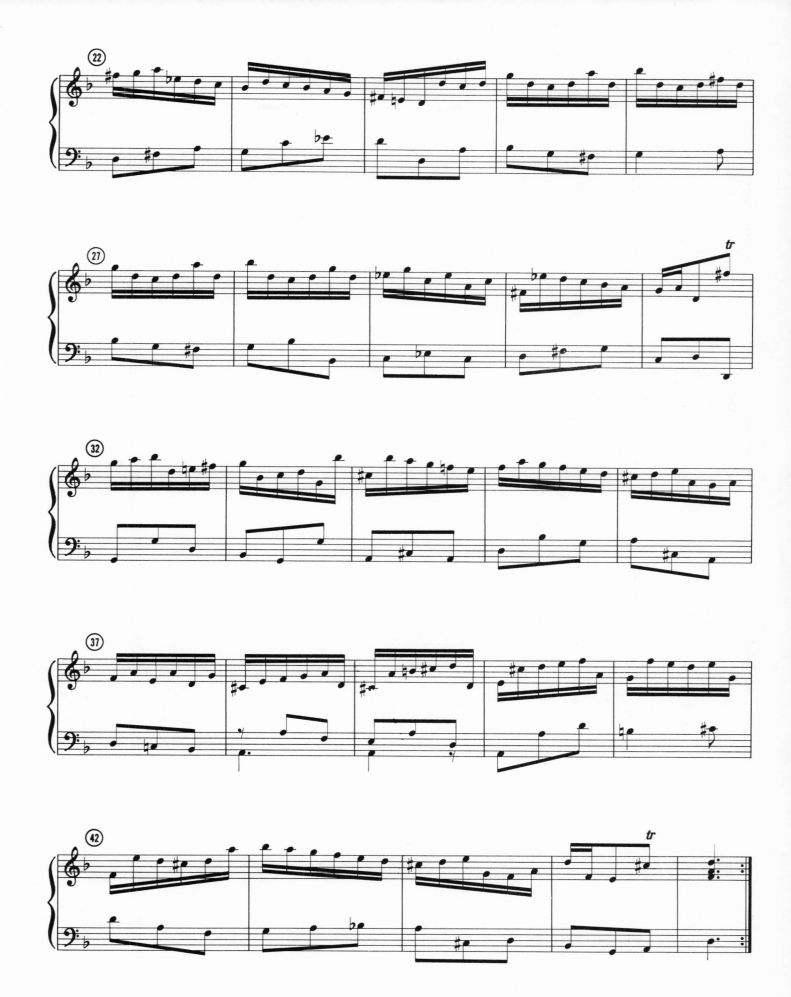

9

GAVOTTES I AND II (MUSETTE)

from *English Suite No. 3*

Bach

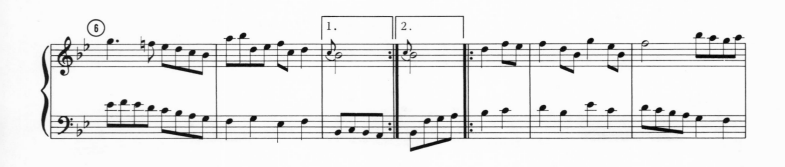

(Gavotte I D.C.)

11

CORRENTE

from *Suite No. 1 for Violoncello Solo*

Bach

GIGUE IN A MINOR

from *Pièces de Clavecin*

Rameau

SONATA IN A MINOR

D. Scarlatti
Kirkpatrick No. 3

17

19

PRELUDE NO. 11 IN F MAJOR

from *The Well-Tempered Clavier, Vol. I*

Bach

INVENTION NO. 4 IN D MINOR

from *The Two-Part Inventions*

Bach

23

INVENTION NO. 13 IN A MINOR

from *The Two-Part Inventions*

Bach

INVENTION NO. 1 IN C MAJOR

from *The Two-Part Inventions*

Bach

INVENTION NO. 6 IN E MAJOR

from *The Two-Part Inventions*

Bach

30

PRELUDE NO. 20 IN A MINOR

from *The Well-Tempered Clavier, Vol. II*

Bach

ADAGIO

from *Sonata No. 1 for Recorder and Continuo*

Handel

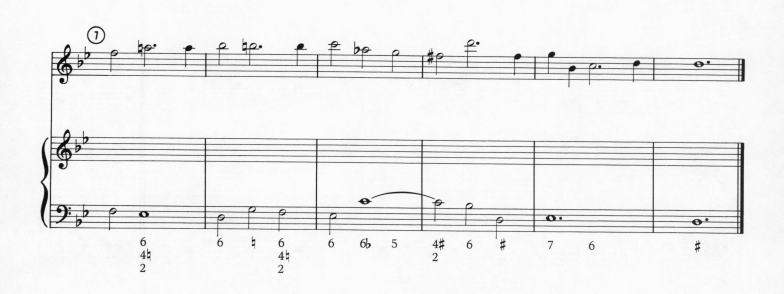

ALLA BREVE

from *Sonata No. 3 for Flute and Continuo*

Handel

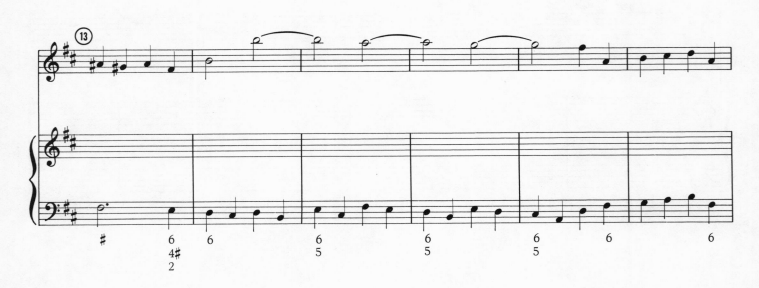

36

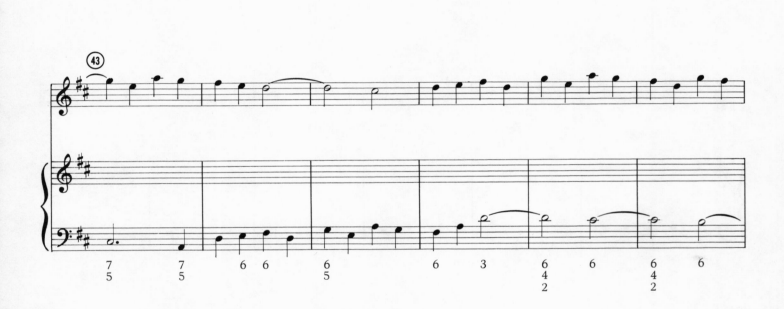

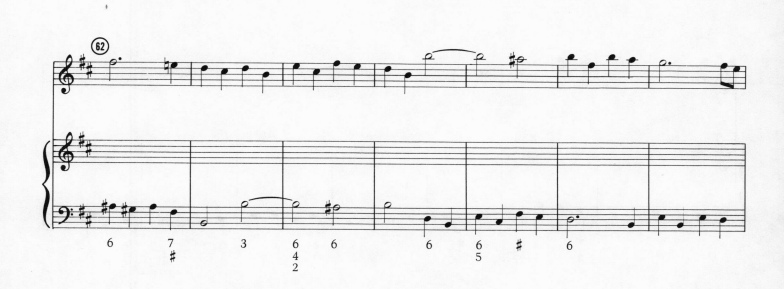

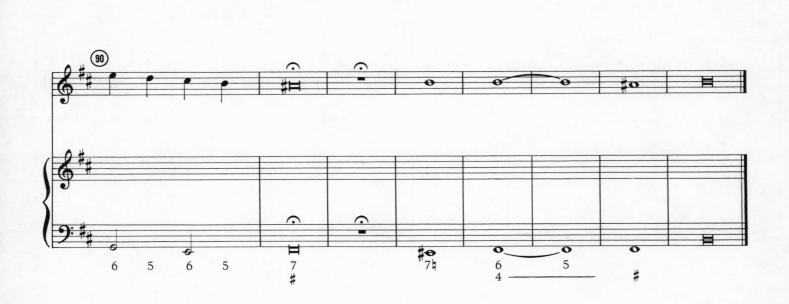

40

SALVE, PACIS NUNTIA

Buxtehude

Sal-ve,_ pa-cis_ nun - ti-a,   i - ris so-lis fi - li-a,   i - ris_ nu-bis_ fi - li-a,

sal - ve, sal-ve,_ coe - li_ gem-mu - la,   sal-ve,_ sal - ve,

From *Dietrich Buxtehude Werke*, Vol. VI.
Copyright 1953 by Ugrino-Verlag, Hamburg. Reprinted by permission.

sal - ve,___ sal - ve,___ sal - ve,___ sal - ve, sal - ve, pa - cis, sal - ve, pa - cis,

sal - ve,___ pa - cis___ nun - ti - a, sal - ve,___ sal - ve,___ sal - ve,___ sal - ve,

sal - ve, pa - cis___ nun - ti - a, sal - ve,___ pa - cis___ nun - ti - a!

Song: AH! AH! AH! MY ANNA

from *Dido and Aeneas*

Purcell

- guish 'till my grief is known, I lan - -

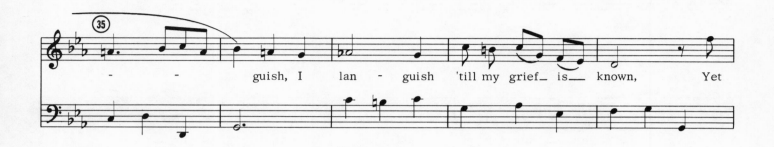

- - guish, I lan - guish 'till my grief_ is_ known, Yet

would not, yet would not, would_ not have_ it guess'd_

_ Peace_ and I are stran - gers,_

grown, Peace_ and I are stran - gers,_ stran - gers_

Violino I

Violino II

Viola

grown.

Basso

CHORALE PRELUDE

Versus III from *Psalmus: Da Jesus an dem Kreuze stand*

Scheidt

BICINIUM

from *Cantio sacra: Warum betrübst du dich, mein Herz*

Scheidt

CANON

from *The Art of Fugue*

Bach

50

51

CANON

Variation 27 from *Aria with 30 Variations* (Goldberg Variations)

Bach

UNIT II

POLYPHONY FROM THE BAROQUE ERA

COUNTERPOINT IN THREE OR MORE PARTS

SUGGESTIONS AND QUESTIONS FOR ANALYSIS AND DISCUSSION

A. Perform the music.
   (Use whatever means are available to the class: piano, other instruments, or voices.)

B. Determine the basic key of the work.
   Point out the principle elements that define the tonality.

C. Examine the rhythmic structure.
   1. Perform each individual voice by clapping or tapping the rhythm. Comment on the rhythmic patterns.
   2. Perform the combined voices rhythmically. What observations can be made about rhythmic drive? cadences? climaxes?

D. Discuss the relationship between the voices.
   1. Motivic
   2. Rhythmic
   3. Directional

E. Outline the formal structure.
   1. Entries, episodes, etc.
   2. Key relationships (Identify and compare the cadences.)
   3. Recurring sections
   4. Other features

F. Study the contrapuntal techniques and discuss the use of compositional devices. (Imitation, invertible counterpoint, sequence, etc.)

G. Analyze the harmony.
   1. Identify the root and quality of each chordal structure.
   2. Using Roman numerals and figured bass symbols, indicate the harmonic function of each chord.
   3. Circle and name the nonharmonic tones.
   4. Locate and explain all modulations.

H. Discuss other significant aspects which lead to an intelligent musical performance.
   1. Rhythm and tempo
   2. High points
   3. Change of texture
   4. Stylistic considerations
   5. Text*

I. Compare works of similar form.
   1. Motivic material
   2. Rhythmic figures
   3. Modulations
   4. Compositional devices
   5. Texture

*Translations appear on pages 322-323.

Handel, *Suite No. 4,* Courante
(A) Harmonic study, modulation

Bach, *Well-Tempered Clavier, Vol. I*, Fugue XVI
(B) Structural and motivic analysis

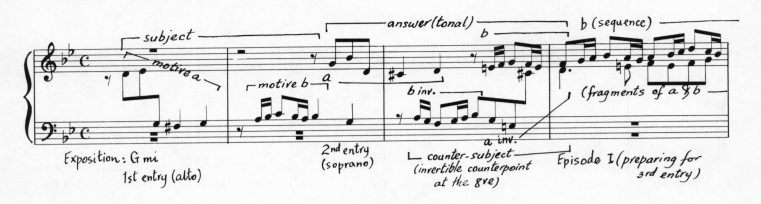

CHORALE AND TWO VARIATIONS

from *Choral mit 8 Partiten: Alle menschen müssen sterben*

From *Pachelbel Organ Collection*, Vol. IV.
Copyright 1936 by Bärenreiter-Verlag, Kassel.   Reprinted by permission.

Partita II

Chorale Prelude: WIR DANKEN DIR, HERR JESU CHRIST

Buxtehude

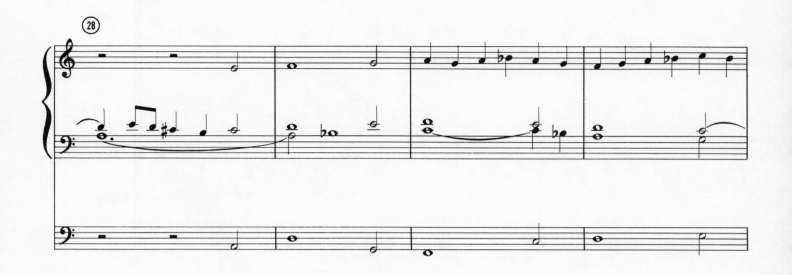

Chorale Prelude: DURCH ADAMS FALL IST GANZ VERDERBT

Buxtehude

Chorale Prelude: VATER UNSER IM HIMMELREICH

from *Orgelbüchlein*

Bach

69

Chorale Prelude: ERSCHIENEN IST DER HERRLICHE TAG

from *Orgelbüchlein*

Bach

71

Chorale Prelude: DURCH ADAMS FALL IST GANZ VERDERBT

from *Orgelbüchlein*

Bach

Compare this work with the chorale prelude on pages 64-67.

73

FRENCH SUITE NO. 1

Bach

Allemande

75

Courante

77

Sarabande

78

Minuet I

Minuet II

Minuet I D.C.

Gigue

84

GIGUE

from *English Suite No. 3*

Bach

86

SARABANDE

from *Suite No. 12*

Handel

THEME AND SIX VARIATIONS

from *Chaconne in G Major*

Handel

Var. 5

Var. 6

Var. 12

Var. 62

PASSACAGLIA

Buxtehude

93

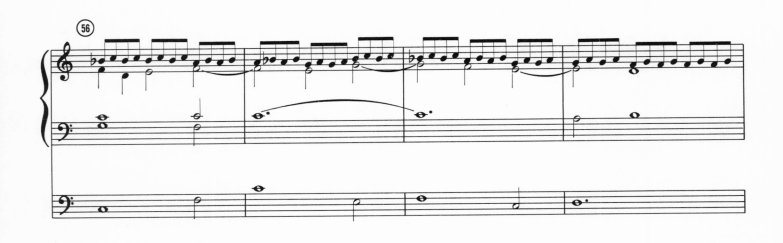

99

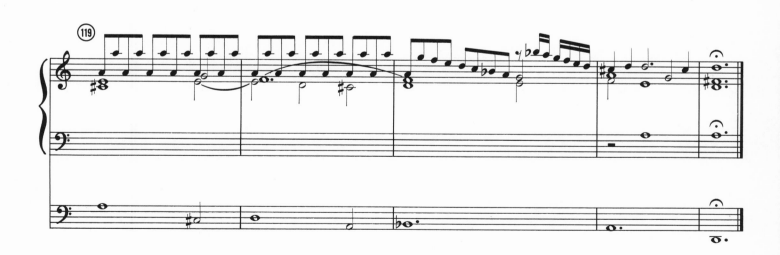

CORRENTE

from *Sonata da Camera a Tre' in D Minor*

Vivaldi

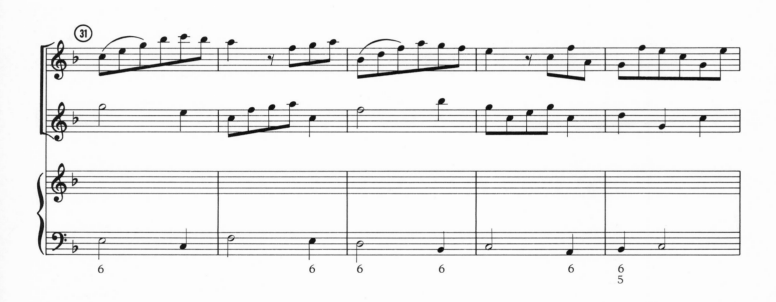

SONATA DA CHIESA A TRE'

Corelli

Adagio

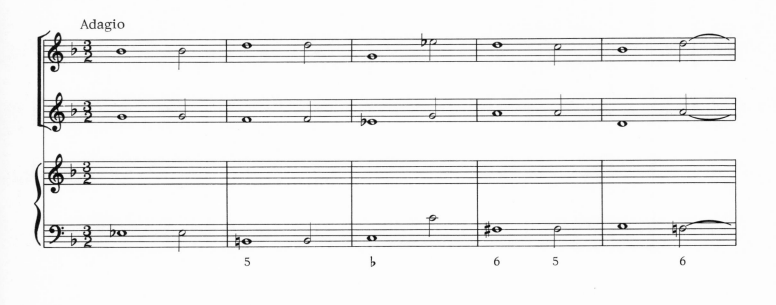

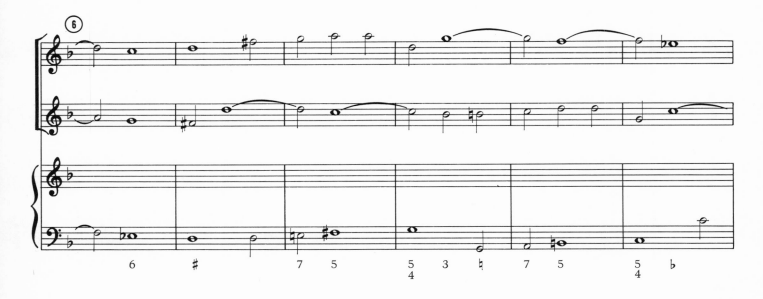

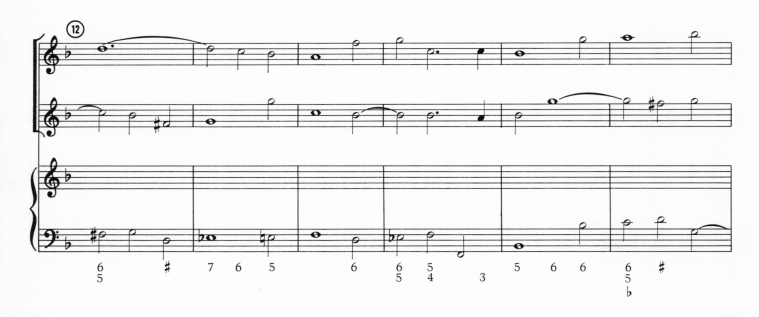

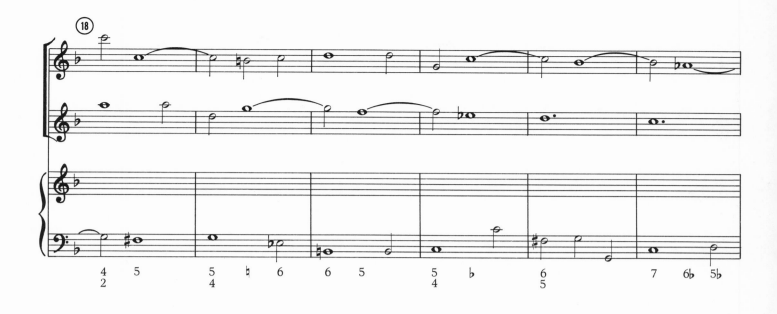

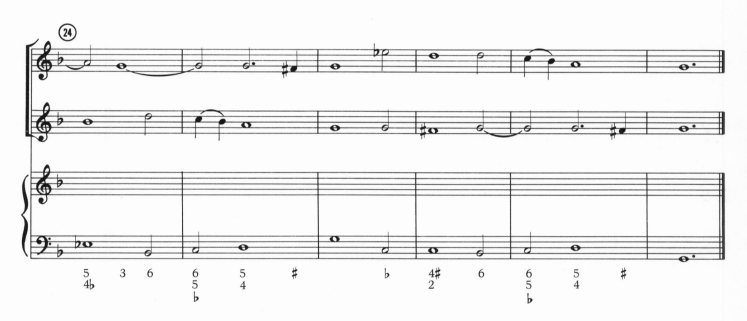

113

114

CANONS

from *The Musical Offering*

Bach

Compare your solutions to these enigmatic canons with those available in many published editions of the above.

III. a 2 Violini in unisono

IV. a 2 Per motum contrarium

Thema

V. a 2 Per augmentationem, contrario motu

Thema

SINFONIA (INVENTION NO. 13) IN A MINOR

from *The Three-Part Inventions*

Bach

CANZONE DOPO L'EPISTOLA

from *Fiori Musicali*

Frescobaldi

122

FUGUE NO. 7 IN E♭ MAJOR

from *The Well-Tempered Clavier, Vol. I*

Bach

126

FUGUE NO. 2 IN C MINOR

from *The Well-Tempered Clavier, Vol. I*

Bach

129

FUGUE NO. 11 IN F MAJOR

from *The Well-Tempered Clavier, Vol. I*

Bach

131

FUGUE NO. 15 IN G MAJOR

from *The Well-Tempered Clavier, Vol. I*

Bach

134

135

136

FUGUE NO. 8 IN D♯ MINOR

from *The Well-Tempered Clavier, Vol. I*

Bach

THREE EXPOSITIONS

from *The Art of Fugue*

Bach

Contrapunctus I

142

Contrapunctus III

Contrapunctus VII

PRELUDE AND FUGUE

No. 10 from *Ariadne Musica*

J.K.F. Fischer

146

FUGUE IN E♭ MAJOR

J.C. Bach

149

FUGUE

Toccata in E Minor, Part II

Bach

Aria: SEUFZER, THRÄNEN, KUMMER, NOTH

from Cantata No. 21, *Ich hatte viel Bekümmernis*

Bach

154

Seuf - zer, Thrän - en, Kum - mer, Noth,___ Seuf-zer, Thrän - en, Kum-mer,

Noth,___ na - gen mein__ be-klemm-tes__ Herz, ich__ em-pfin - de Jam - mer,

D. S. al Fine

Schmerz Seuf - zer, Thrän - en, Kum - mer, Kum-mer, Noth!

D. S. al Fine

Recitative and Chorus: **WIR HABEN KEINE KÖNIG**

from *St. John Passion*

Schütz

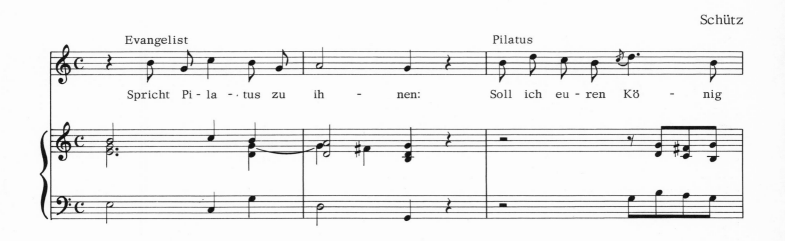

Spricht Pi - la - tus zu ih - nen: Soll ich eu - ren Kö - nig

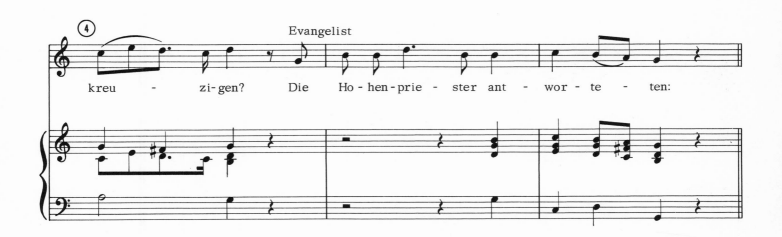

kreu - zi - gen? Die Ho - hen - prie - ster ant - wor - te - ten:

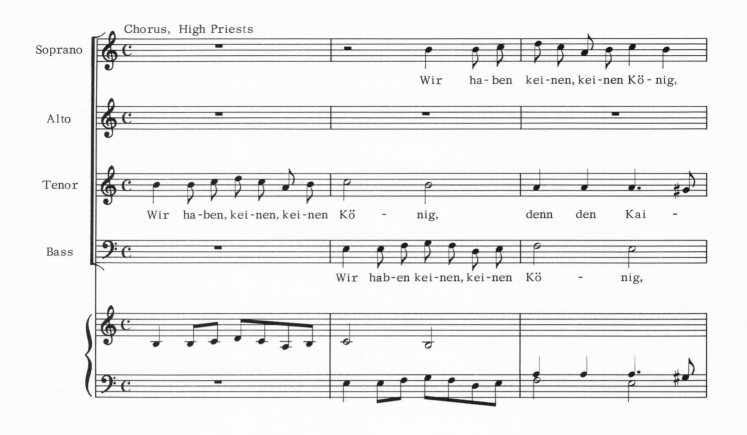

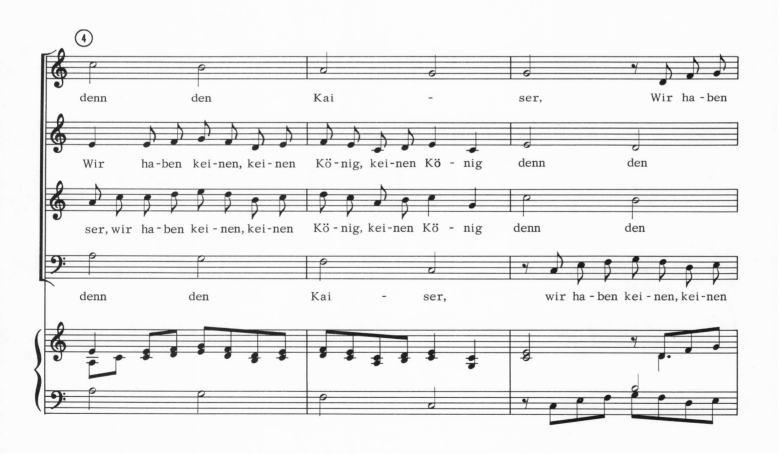

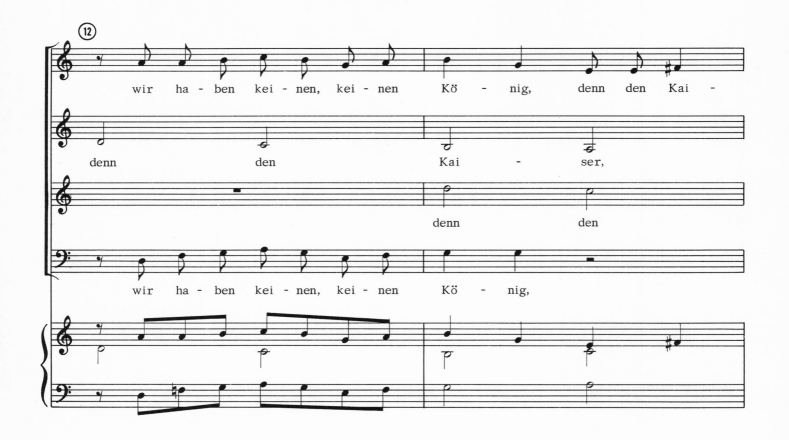

wir ha-ben kei-nen, kei-nen Kö - nig, denn den Kai -

denn den Kai - ser,

denn den

wir ha-ben kei-nen, kei-nen Kö - nig,

ser, denn _____ den Kai - ser!

wir ha-ben kei-nen, kei-nen Kö - nig, denn _____ den Kai - ser!

Kai - ser, denn den Kai - ser!

denn den Kai - - ser!

SINFONIA AND VERSE

from Cantata No. 4, *Christ lag in Todesbanden*

Bach

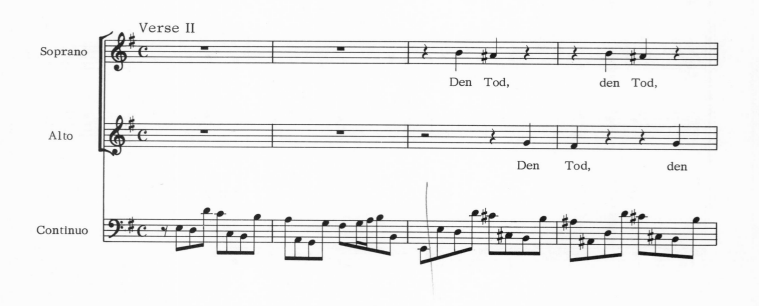

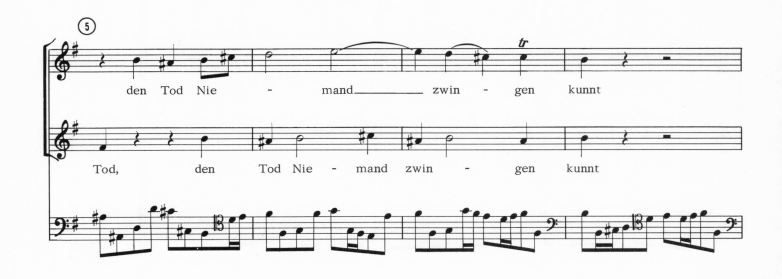

den Tod Nie - mand zwin - gen kunnt

Tod, den Tod Nie - mand zwin - gen kunnt

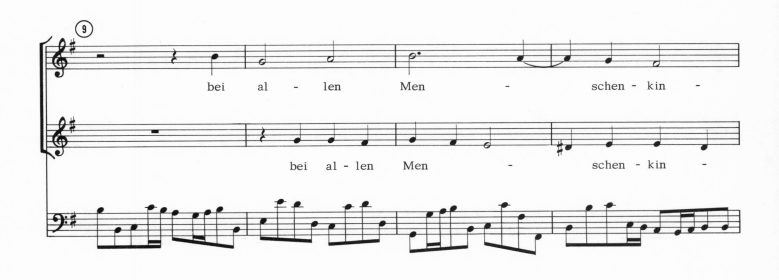

bei al - len Men - schen kin -

bei al - len Men - schen kin -

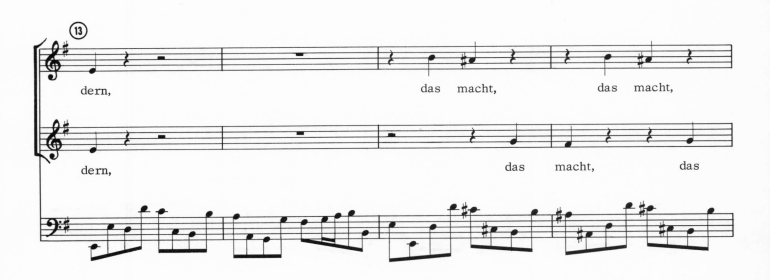

dern, das macht, das macht,

dern, das macht, das

das macht al - les_____ un - ser Sünd',

macht, das macht al - les un - ser Sünd',

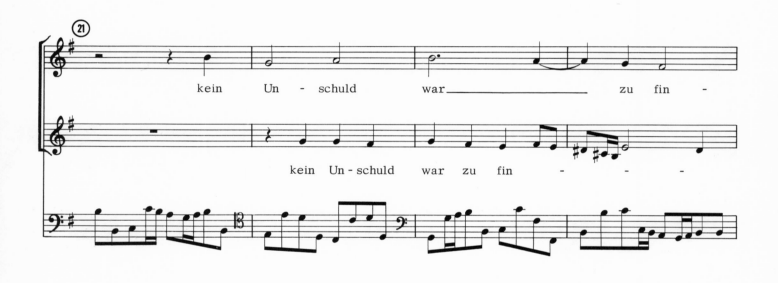

kein Un - schuld war_____ zu fin -

kein Un - schuld war zu fin - - -

den. Da von kam_____ der Tod,

den. Da von kam der

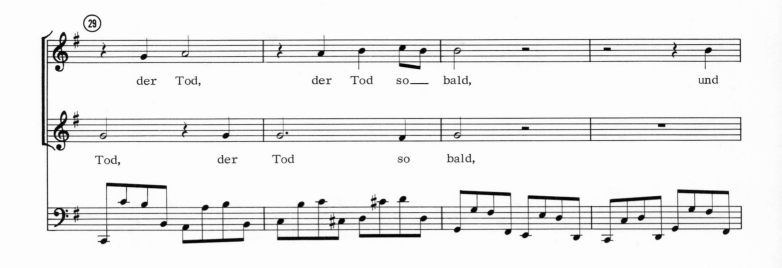

der Tod, der Tod so bald, und

Tod, der Tod so bald,

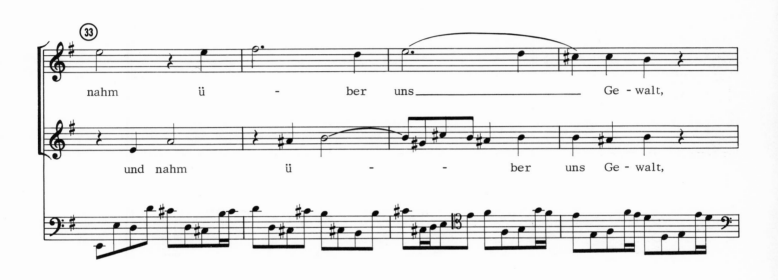

nahm ü - ber uns   Ge - walt,

und nahm ü - - ber uns Ge - walt,

hielt uns in sei - nem

hielt uns in sei - nem Reich ge -

Reich ge-fan - gen, ge-fan - gen. Hal - le -
fan - gen, ge-fan - gen. Hal - le -

lu - jah, hal - le - lu - jah, hal -
- lu - jah, hal - le - lu - jah, hal -

- le - lu - jah, hal - le - lu - jah!_____
le - lu - jah, hal - le - lu - jah!_____

Chorus: DEIN ALTER SEI WIE DEINE JUGEND

from Cantata No. 71, *Gott ist mein König*

Bach

168

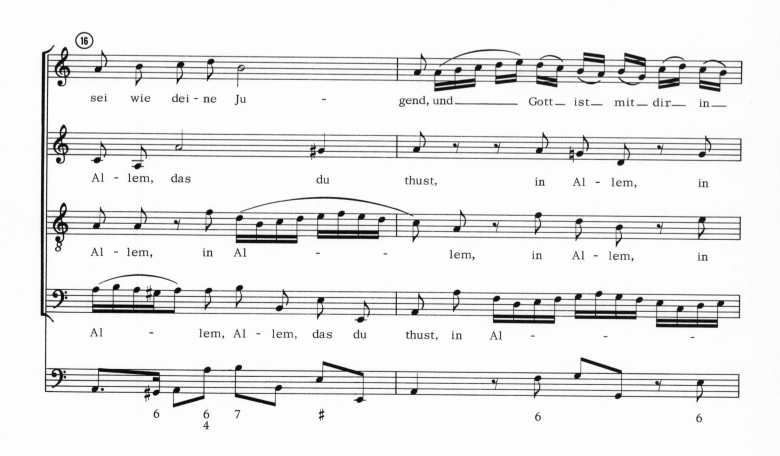

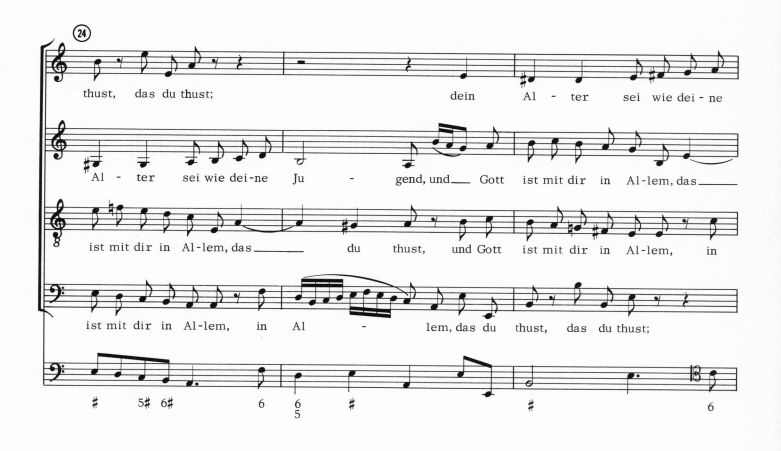

in Al -
lem, das du thust,

Al - lem, das du thust, in Al - - - - - - -

Al - lem, das du thust, und Gott ist mit dir in

- lem, das du thust, und Gott ist mit dir in Al - lem, in

7   7   7   6   7   6

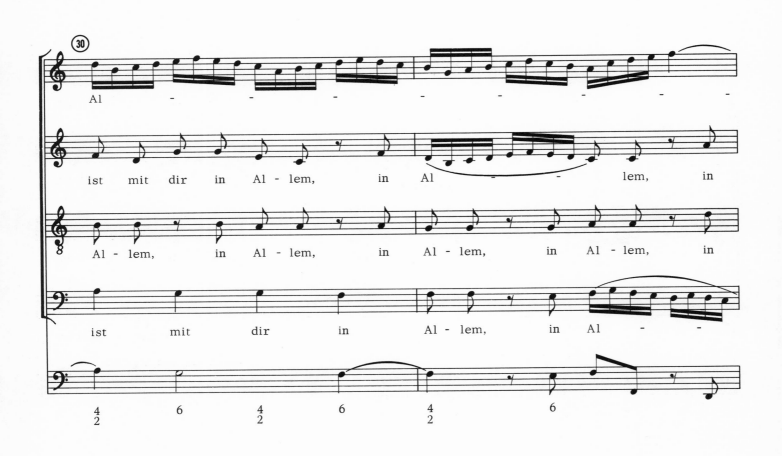

Al - - - - - - - - -

ist mit dir in Al - lem, in Al - - lem, in

Al - lem, in Al - lem, in Al - lem, in Al - lem, in

ist mit dir in Al - lem, in Al - -

4/2   6   4/2   6   4/2   6

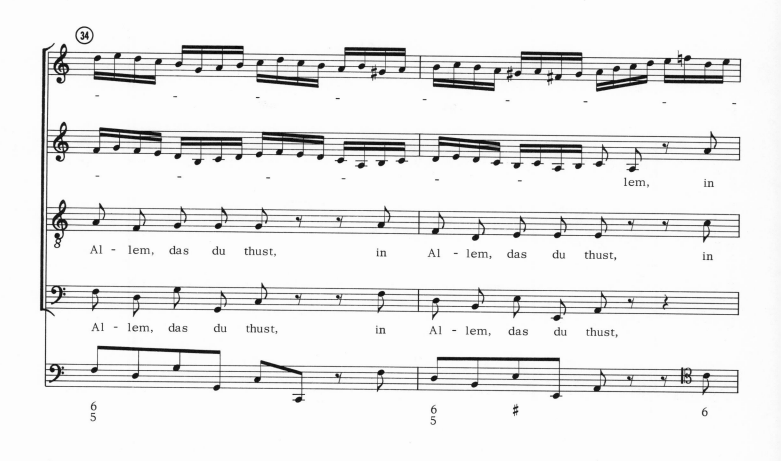

ALLEGRO

from *Concerto Grosso in D Minor*, Third Movement

Handel

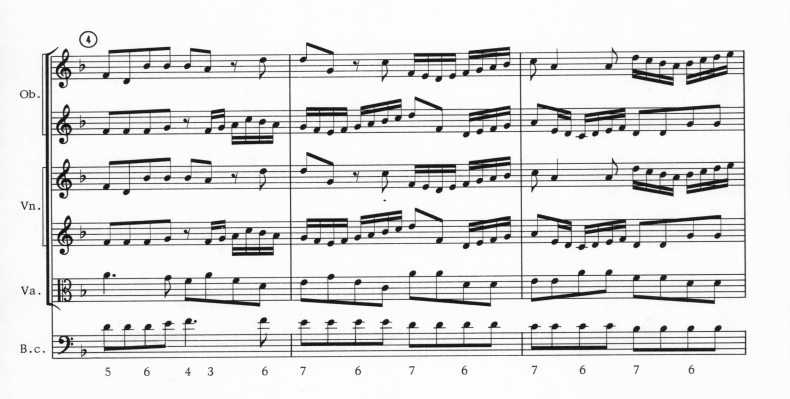

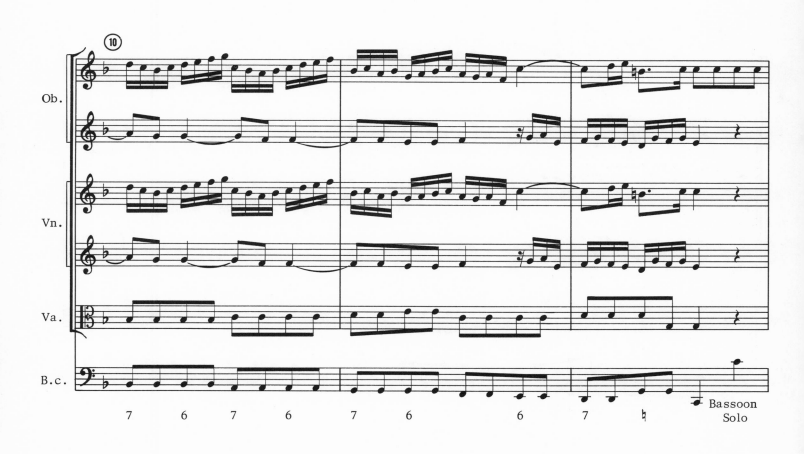

175

176

Bassoon Solo

179

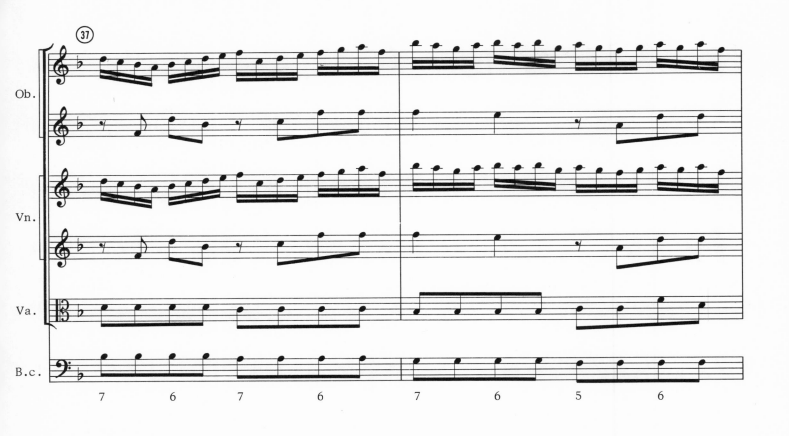

180

UNIT III

POLYPHONY FROM THE SIXTEENTH CENTURY

COUNTERPOINT IN TWO PARTS

A. Sing and analyze each melodic line.
    1. Analyze the melodic curves, range, high points and points of rest of each line.
    2. Discuss the presence of conjunct and disjunct motion.
    3. What kinds of intervals are used melodically? What melodic intervals seem to be avoided? How are large leaps handled?
    4. How long is each phrase? Compare the phrases. Analyze the cadences.
    5. What other melodic features have you observed (recurring melodic figures, use of musica ficta, etc)?

B. Analyze each voice rhythmically.
    (*Note:* In some of the works, the original rhythmic notation has been halved.)
    1. Analyze the rhythmic structure of each phrase. What kinds of notes appear frequently? What kinds are used sparingly? What note values seem to be avoided?
    2. Point out some characteristic rhythmic patterns. Note the relative rhythmic activity at the beginning, middle, and end of the phrase.
    3. What observations can be made about rhythm and metric variety? Since bar lines were not used in this period, how can beginnings and ends of phrases, metric units, and accents be determined?
    4. Compare the rhythm of this period with that of the Baroque era; with other periods in music history.

C. Analyze the relationship between the lines.
    1. Sing or play the music.
    2. Perform and write out the rhythmic patterns formed by combining the parts. What observations can you make regarding rhythmic interplay between the voices and the over-all rhythmic flow?
    3. How does the composer create unity between the parts (imitation, inversion, other compositional devices)?
    4. Name the intervals formed by the parts. What intervals appear most frequently?
    5. What conclusions can you draw about the frequency and location of consonant intervals?
    6. Circle and identify the dissonant intervals. How are they handled rhythmically? How are they resolved?
    7. Examine the cadences. What are the characteristic intervals, chords, dissonances, and special rhythmic patterns?
    8. What other features do you observe about the work (texture, use of "familiar" style, etc.)?

D. Study the text. *
    1. How is the general mood of the text expressed in the music?
    2. How are important words or phrases highlighted (use of rhythm, large leaps, melismatic passages, etc.)?
    3. How are individual words set (rhythmic consideration, accent, relation to melodic shape)?
    4. To what extent is the form of the work generated by the text?

E. After analyzing several works from this unit, what conclusions about style can be noted?
    1. Rhythm
    2. Modality
    3. Phrase structure
    4. Form
    5. Notation
    6. Text setting

F. What influence can your analysis have on the performance of the work?

*Translations appear on pages 321-324.

Palestrina, Sanctus from *Missa Sine Nomine*
(A) Melodic study

San - ctus, san - - - ctus

San - ctus, san - - - ctus, san -

etc.

etc.

Mode: Lower voice begins in Aeolian, cadences in Ionian (m. 5-6). Upper voice, which imitates a 5th higher after one measure (but, see the F natural), begins in Phrygian.

Rhythm: Starts with longer note values, activity increases in m. 3-4, slight slowing down (for cadence) m. 5.

Text: First statement of sanctus is on a repeated note, the accented syllable (sán-ctus) gets the longer value; second statement has a long melisma on the first syllable.

Shape: Lower voice starts with a repeated A, leaps a 3rd, descends to A filling in gap, then by step up to D, down a step, up by step to F (high point) then descends by step to C (cadence), etc. Range is a 6th. The movement is predominantly by step.

Upper voice (imitation) has the same shape

Lines in combination: m. 1-3   oblique and contrary motions predominate
                        m. 4-5   similar motion (in 3rds)
                        m. 5-6   oblique and contrary motions (at the cadence)

Lassus, excerpt from *Aegra Currit*

(B) Intervalic study, non-harmonic tones

All dissonances are on weak beats except for the suspensions

CONTRAPUNTAL STUDY

from *Composition Regeln*

Sweelinck

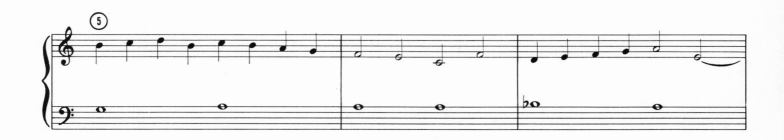

CONTRAPUNTAL STUDY

from *Composition Regeln*

Sweelinck

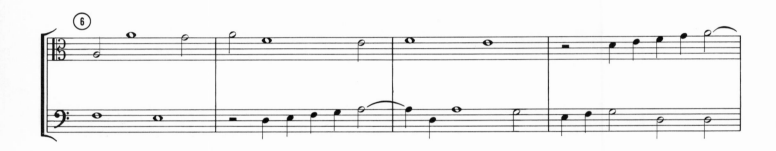

CONTRAPUNTAL STUDY

from *Composition Regeln*

Sweelinck

SUB DIVERSIS SPECIEBUS

from *Lauda, Sion, Salvatorem*

Brumel

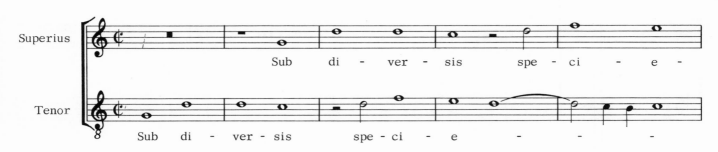

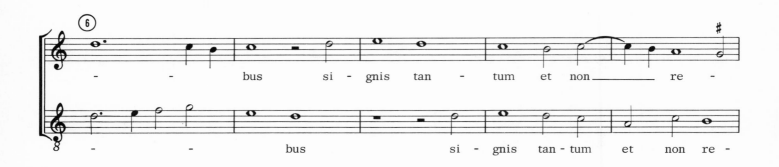

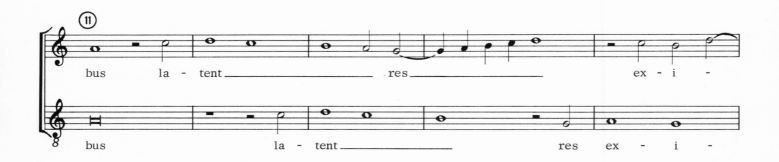

From *Van Ockeghem tot Sweelinck*, Vol. VI, Dr. A. Smijers, ed.
Copyright 1951 by G. Alsbach & Co., Amsterdam. Reprinted by permission.

IN NOMINE

from *Missa: Gaudeamus*

Josquin des Prez

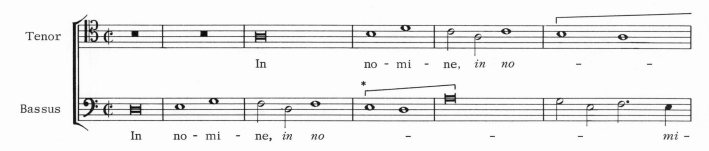

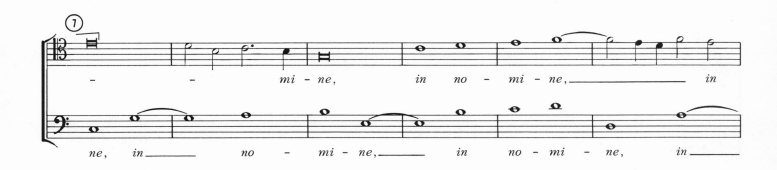

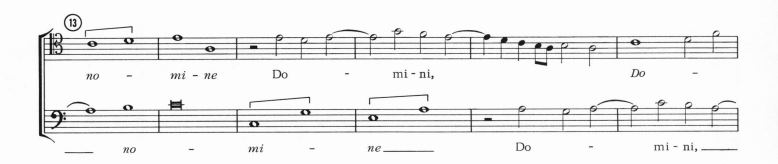

From *Werken van Josquin des Prez,* Vol. 12.
Copyright 1927 by G. Alsbach & Co., Amsterdam. Reprinted by permission.

* The bracket (⌐⎯⎯⎯⎯⎯⎯⎯¬) indicates the presence in the original of a ligature, a symbol representing two or more successive notes.

PLENI SUNT COELI

from *Missa: L'Homme armé*

Josquin des Prez

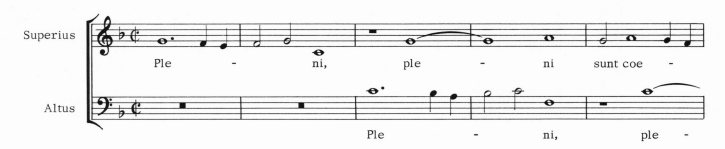

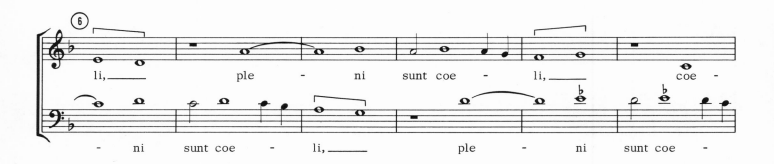

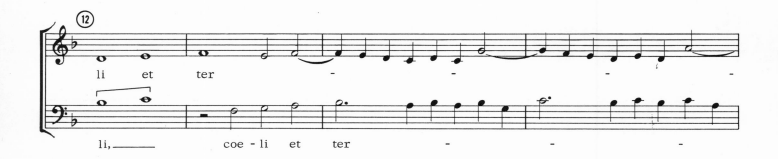

From *Werken van Josquin des Prez*, Vol. 14.
Copyright 1931 by Fr. Kistner & C.F.W. Siegel, Leipzig. Reprinted by permission.

AVE MARIA

Tract from *Annunciationis Mariae* in *Choralis Constantinus*

Isaac

From *Denkmäler der Tonkunst in Österreich*, Vol. 10, 1898.
Published by Akademische Druck-u. Verlagsanstalt, Graz, Austria. Used by permission.

Motet: OCULUS NON VIDIT

from *Cantiones Duarum Vocum*

Lassus

Motet: JUSTUS COR SUUM TRADET

from *Cantiones Duarum Vocum*

Lassus

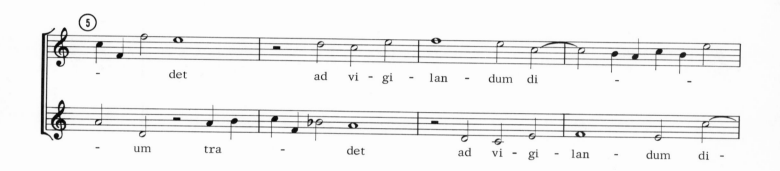

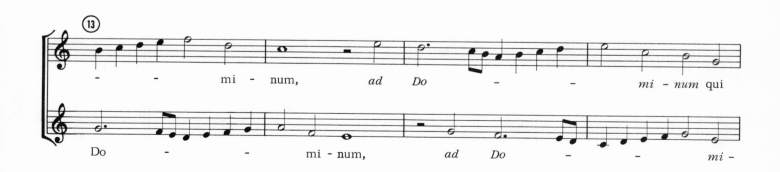

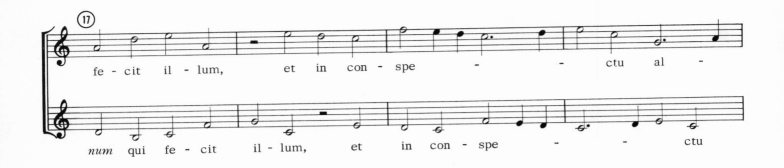

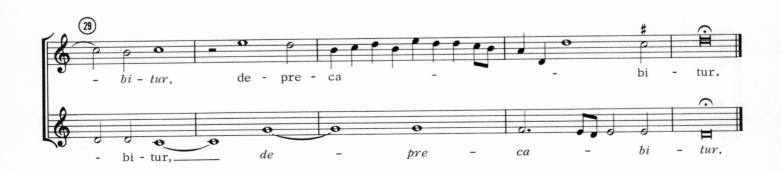

Motet: QUI SEQUITUR ME

from *Cantiones Duarum Vocum*

Lassus

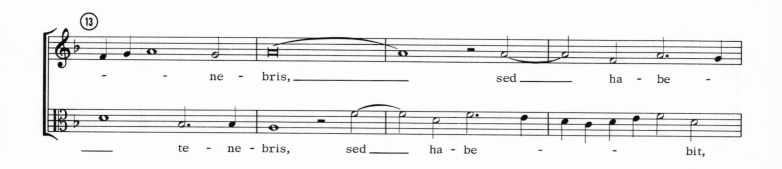

Frottola: AMOR CHE MI CONSIGLI?

Festa

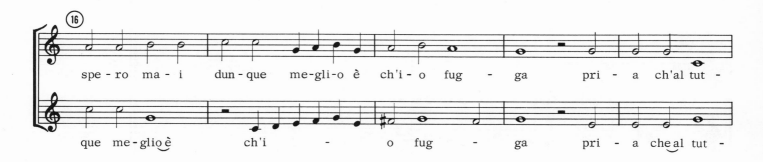

Canzonet: FIRE AND LIGHTNING

Morley

Fire and light - ning from heav'n fall, fire and light - ning from heav'n

Fire and light - ning from heav'n fall, fire and light -

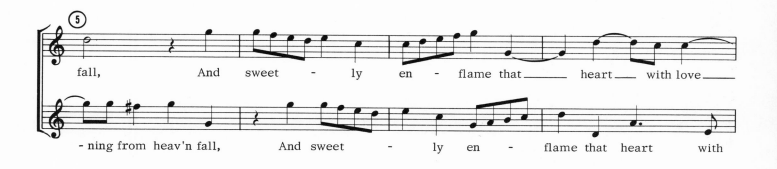

fall, And sweet - ly en - flame that____ heart__ with love____

- ning from heav'n fall, And sweet - ly en - flame that heart with

____ a - right - ful, Fire and light - ning from heav'n fall, fire and light - ning from

love a - right - ful, Fire and light - ning from heav'n fall, fire

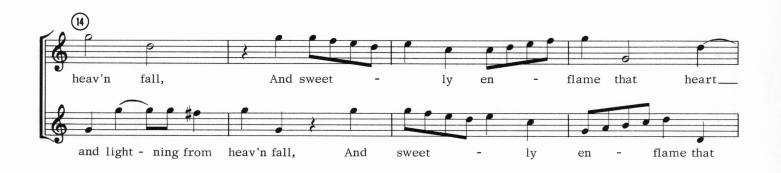

heav'n fall, And sweet - ly en - flame that heart__

and light - ning from heav'n fall, And sweet - ly en - flame that

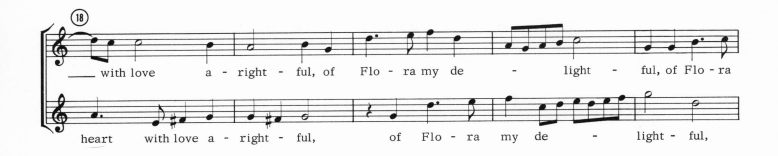

_____ with love a - right - ful, of Flo - ra my de - light - ful, of Flo - ra

heart with love a - right - ful, of Flo - ra my de - light - ful,

my de - light - ful, of Flo - ra my de - light -

of Flo - ra my de - light - ful, of Flo - ra my de -

- ful, so fair but yet so _ spite - ful. Of Flo - ra my de - -

light - ful, so fair but yet _____ so spite - ful. Of Flo - ra my de -

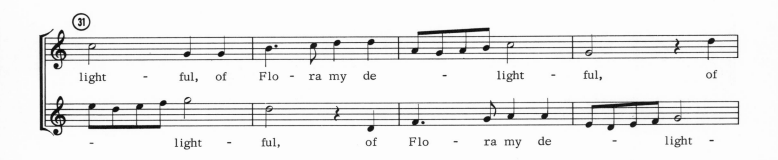

light - ful, of Flo - ra my de - light - ful, of

- light - ful, of Flo - ra my de - light -

Flo - ra my de - light - ful, so fair but yet so spite - ful.

ful, of Flo - ra my de - light - ful, so fair but yet so spite - ful.

200

UNIT IV

POLYPHONY FROM THE SIXTEENTH CENTURY

COUNTERPOINT IN THREE OR MORE PARTS

SUGGESTIONS AND QUESTIONS FOR ANALYSIS AND DISCUSSION

A. Sing and analyze each melodic line.
  1. Analyze the melodic curves, range, high points and points of rest of each line.
  2. Discuss the presence of conjunct and disjunct motion.
  3. What kinds of intervals are used melodically? What melodic intervals seem to be avoided? How are large leaps handled?
  4. How long is each phrase? Compare the phrases. Analyze the cadences.
  5. What other melodic features have you observed (recurring melodic figures, use of musica ficta, etc)?

B. Analyze each voice rhythmically.
  (*Note:* in some of the works, the original rhythmic notation has been halved.)
  1. Analyze the rhythmic structure of each phrase. What kinds of notes appear frequently? What kinds are used sparingly? What note values seem to be avoided?
  2. Point out some characteristic rhythmic patterns. Note the relative rhythmic activity at the beginning, middle, and end of the phrase.
  3. What observations can be made about rhythm and metric variety? Since bar lines were not used in this period, how can beginnings and ends of phrases, metric units, and accents be determined?
  4. Compare the rhythm of this period with that of the Baroque era; with other periods in music history.

C. Analyze the relationship between the lines.
  1. Sing or play the music.
  2. Perform and write out the rhythmic patterns formed by combining the parts. What observations can you make regarding rhythmic interplay between the voices and the over-all rhythmic flow?
  3. How does the composer create unity between the parts (imitation, inversion, other compositional devices)?

D. Analyze the harmony.
  1. Name the intervals formed by the parts. What intervals appear most frequently?
  2. Identify the chord structures. What is the root of each chord?
  3. What is the intervallic relationship between the roots of each chord (up a second, down a fifth, etc.).
  4. Examine the cadences. What are the characteristic intervals, chords, dissonances, and special rhythmic patterns?

E. Study the text.*
  1. How is the general mood of the text expressed in the music?
  2. How are important words or phrases highlighted (use of rhythm, large leaps, melismatic passages, etc.)?
  3. How are individual words set (rhythmic consideration, accent, relation to melodic shape)?
  4. To what extent is the form of the work generated by the text?

*Translations appear on pages 321-322, 324-325.

202

F. After analyzing several works from this unit, what conclusions about style can be noted?
   1. Rhythm
   2. Modality
   3. Phrase structure
   4. Form
   5. Notation
   6. Text setting
   7. Texture

G. What influence can your analysis have on the performance of the work?

Victoria, excerpt from *Missa: Ave, maris stella*
Structural analysis, rhythmic study

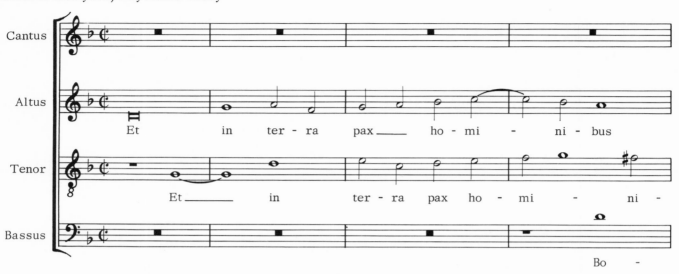

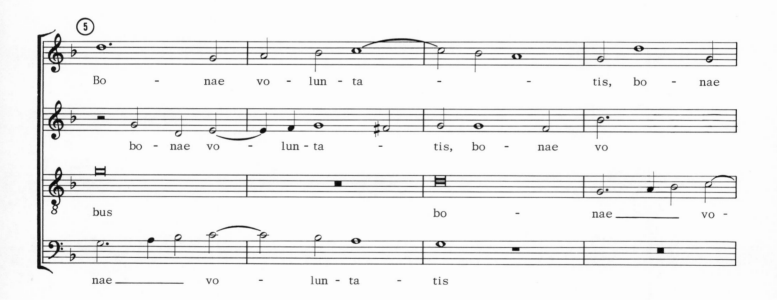

Observations:

1. Tenor imitates alto after two beats (half notes). Note leap of 5th in tenor (tonal answer).

2. Elided cadence at "measure" five as bass and cantus enter in canon at the octave.

3. Alto joins in imitation (note leap of fourth down) one beat after the cantus.

4. Tenor imitates in "measure" seven.

5. See rhythmic study following:

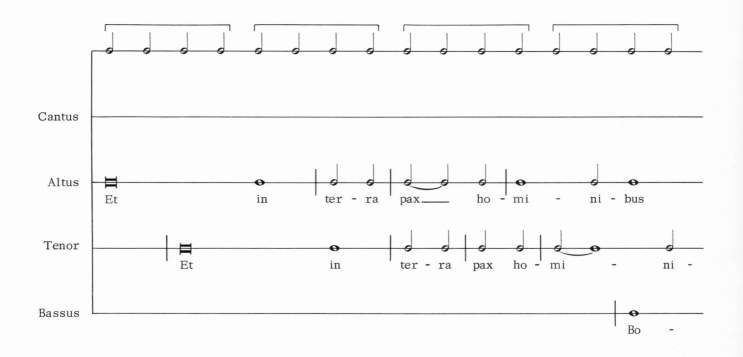

Cantus

Altus

Et in ter - ra pax__ ho - mi - ni - bus

Tenor

Et in ter - ra pax ho - mi - ni -

Bassus

Bo -

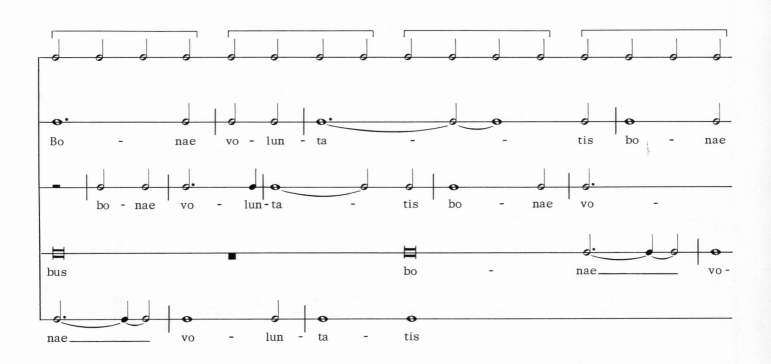

Bo - nae vo - lun - ta - - tis bo - nae

bo - nae vo - lun - ta - tis bo - nae vo -

bus bo - nae__ vo -

nae__ vo - lun - ta - tis

AGNUS DEI

from *Missa ad Fugam*

Josquin des Prez

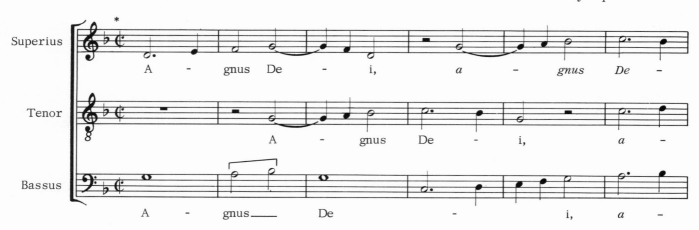

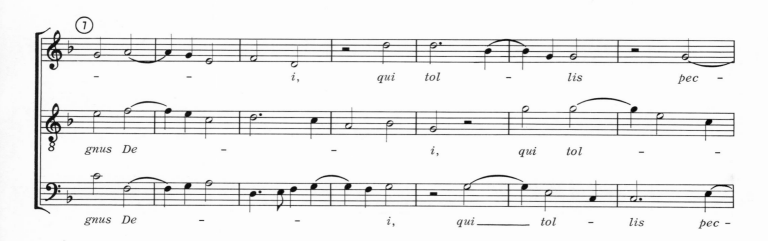

*Notation is halved.

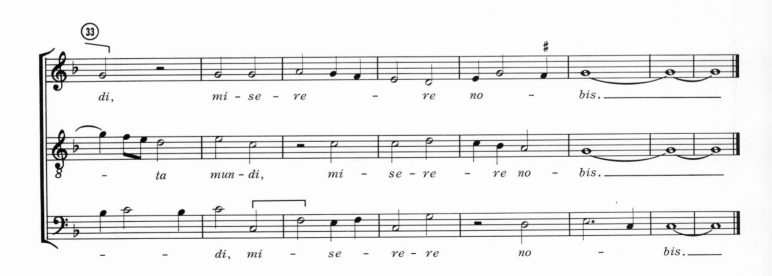

CHRISTE ELEISON

from *Missa: Laetatus*

Victoria

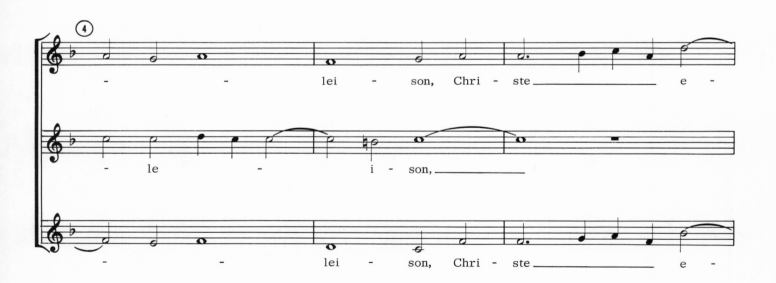

From *Thomae Ludovici Victoria Opera Omnia*, Tomus VI.
Copyright 1909 by Breitkopf & Härtel, Leipzig; Associated Music Publishers, Inc., New York, agents. Reprinted by permission.

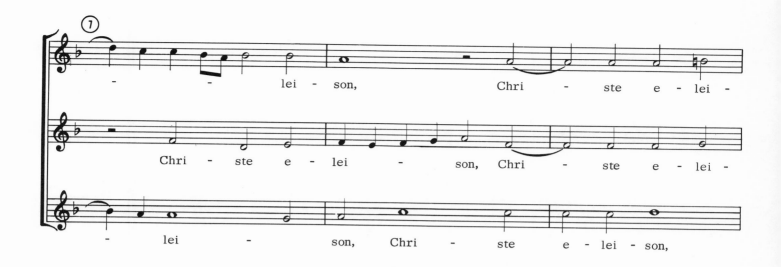

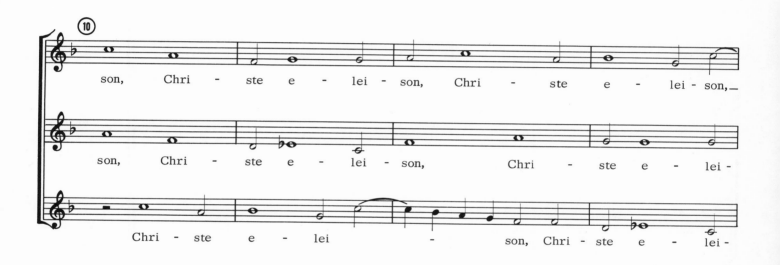

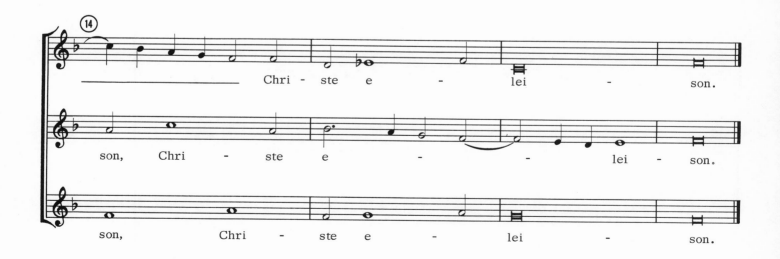

Motet: LAUDABO NOMEN DEI

Lassus

PARS MEA DOMINUS

from *Lamentationum*

Palestrina

From *Le Opere di Giovanni Pierluigi da Palestrina*, Vol. XIII.
Copyright 1941 by Edizioni Fratelli Scalera. Permission granted by Instituto Italiano per la Storia della Musica, Rome.

Madrigal: AWAY, THOU SHALT NOT LOVE ME

Wilbye

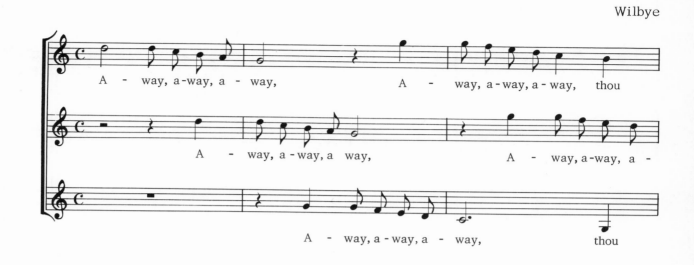

A - way, a-way, a - way,　　　A - way, a-way, a-way,　thou

A - way, a-way, a way,　　　A - way, a-way, a -

A - way, a-way, a - way,　　　thou

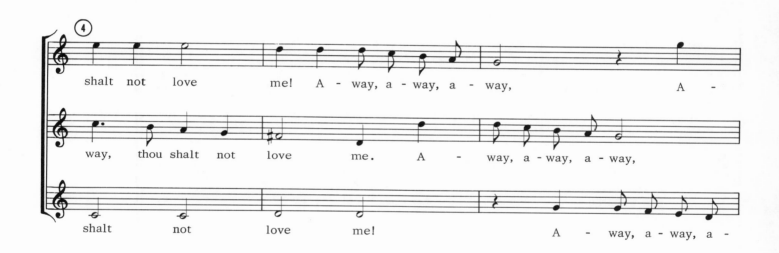

shalt not love　me! A - way, a-way, a - way,　　　A -

way, thou shalt not love　me.　A - way, a-way, a - way,

shalt not love me!　　　A - way, a - way, a -

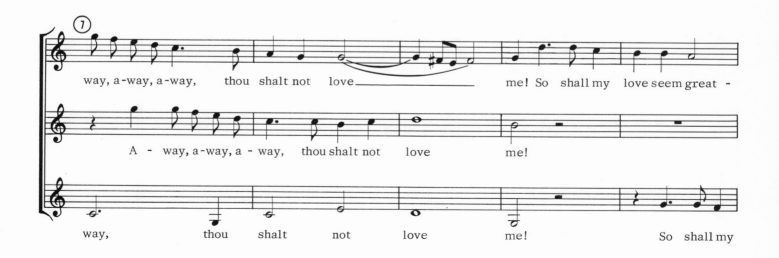

way, a-way, a-way,　thou shalt not love_____ me! So shall my love seem great -

A - way, a-way, a - way, thou shalt not love　me!

way,　thou shalt not love　me!　　　So shall my

er, so shall my love seem great - er, So shall my

So shall my love seem great - er, And I shall love, And I shall love thee bet -

love seem great - er, And I shall love thee bet - ter,

love seem great - er, So shall my love seem great - er, And I shall

ter, So shall my love seem great - er, And I shall love thee bet -

So shall my love seem great - er, And I shall love thee bet - ter, And I shall

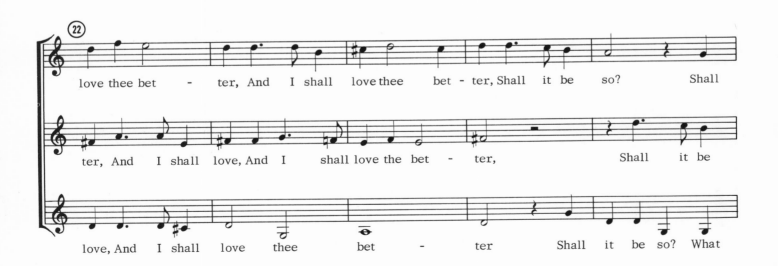

love thee bet - ter, And I shall love thee bet - ter, Shall it be so? Shall

ter, And I shall love, And I shall love the bet - ter, Shall it be

love, And I shall love thee bet - ter Shall it be so? What

214

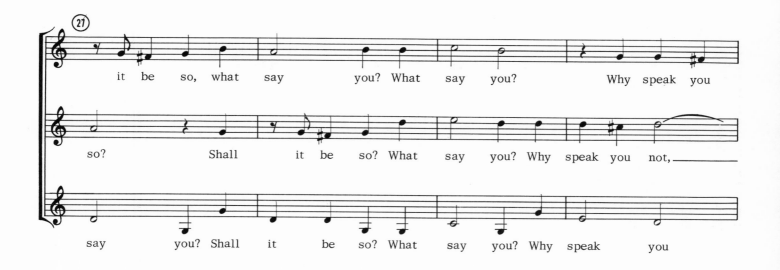

it be so, what say you? What say you? Why speak you

so? Shall it be so? What say you? Why speak you not, _____

say you? Shall it be so? What say you? Why speak you

not, why speak you not, I pray you? Nay then I

_____ why speak you not, I pray you? Nay then _____ I know _____

not, I pray you? Nay then I know you ₁love

know you love me, you love me, Nay then _____ I know you

_____ you _____ love me, Nay then I know you _____ love _____

me, you love me, Nay then _____ I know you love me, you

215

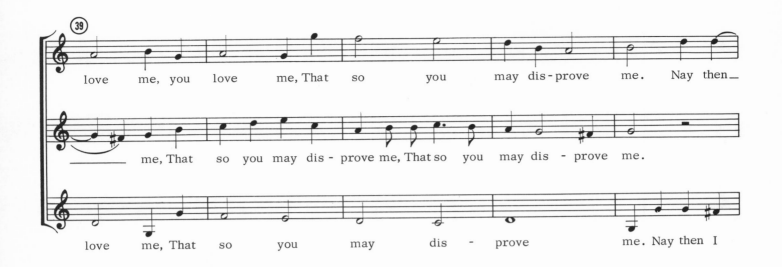

HOSANNA IN EXCELSIS

from *Missa: L'Homme armé*

Josquin des Prez

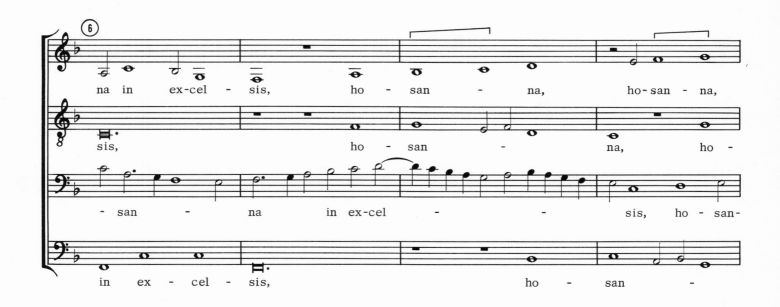

From *Werken van Josquin des Prez*, Vol. 14.
Copyright 1931 by Fr. Kistner & C.F.W. Siegel, Leipzig. Reprinted by permission.

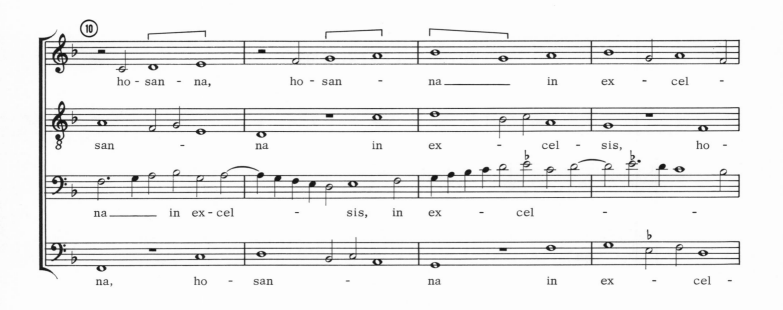

ho - san - na, ho - san - na _____ in ex - cel -

san - na in ex - cel - sis, ho -

na _____ in ex - cel - sis, in ex - cel - -

na, ho - san - na in ex - cel -

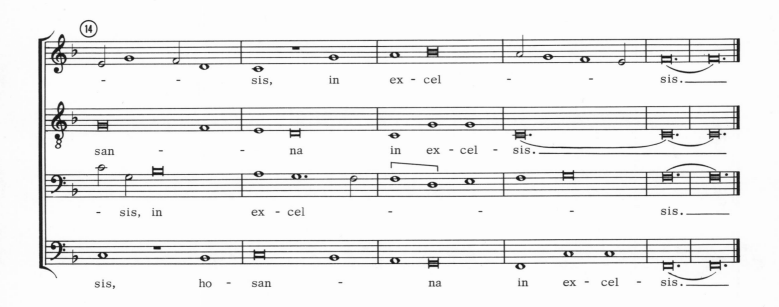

- - sis, in ex - cel - - sis. _____

san - na in ex - cel - sis. _____

- sis, in ex - cel - - - sis. _____

sis, ho - san - na in ex - cel - sis. _____

KYRIE

from *Missa ad Fugam*

Palestrina

*Notation is halved.

Motet: O MAGNUM MYSTERIUM

Victoria

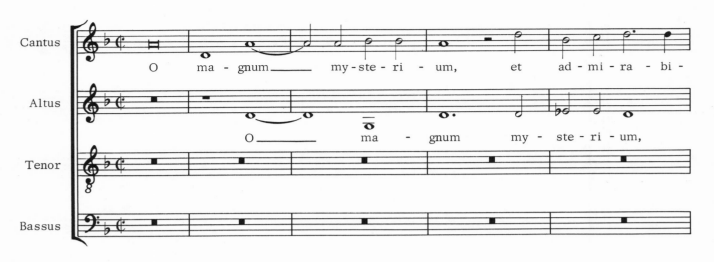

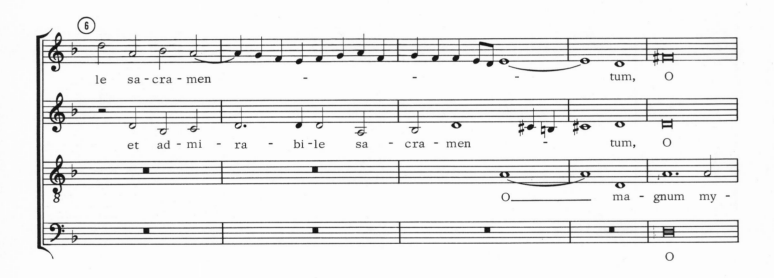

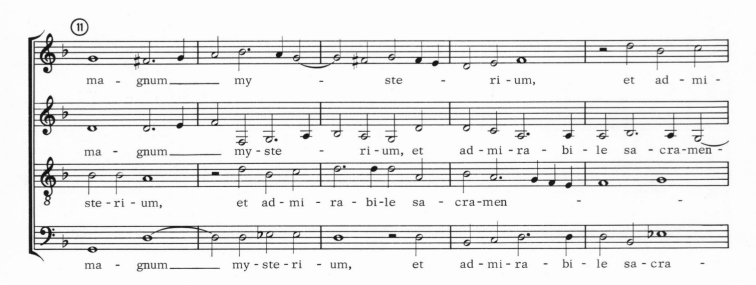

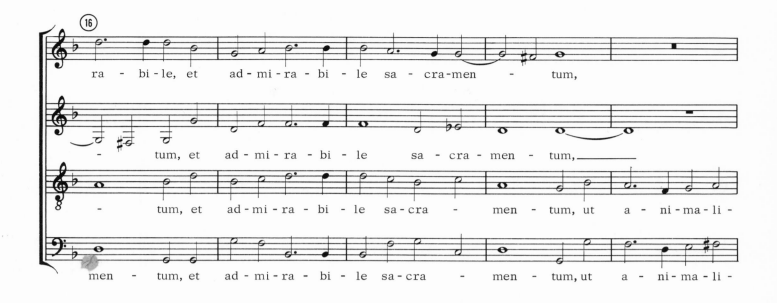

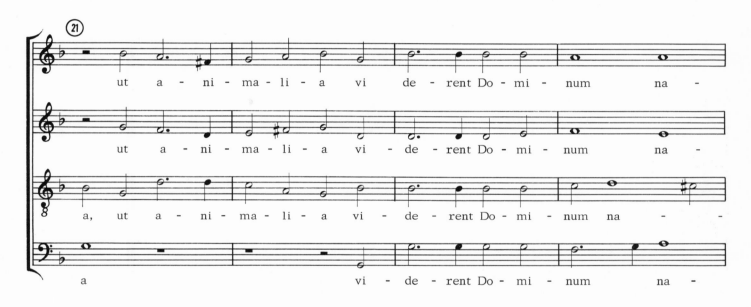

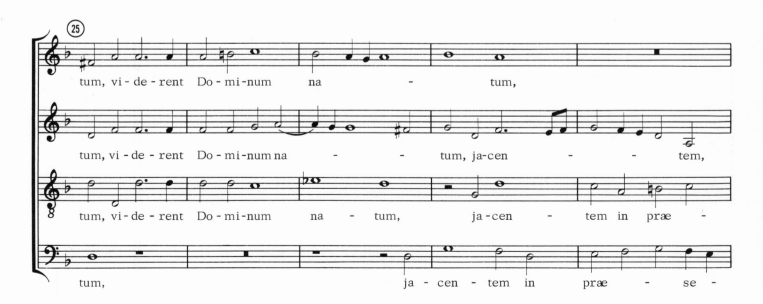

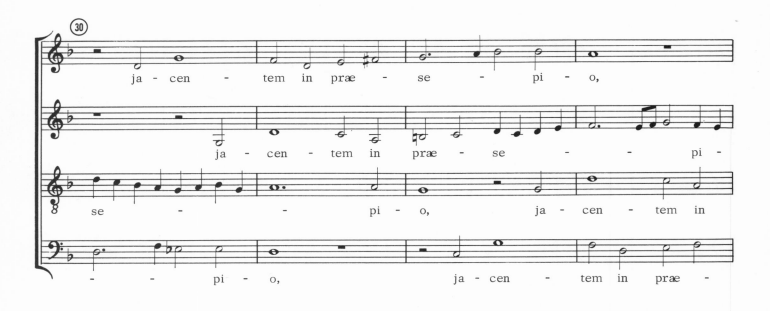

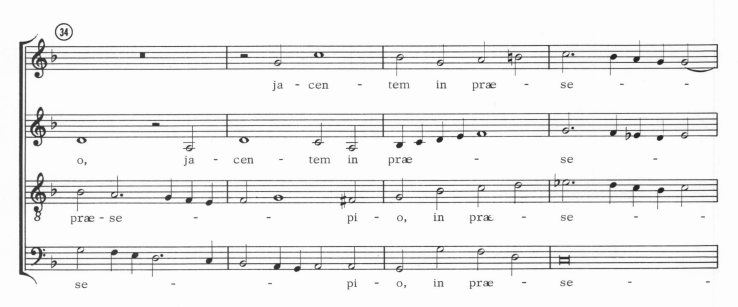

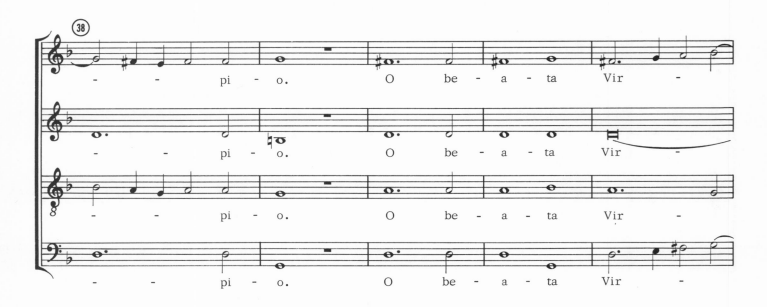

- go, cu - jus vi - sce-ra me - ru - e -
- go, cu - jus vi - sce-ra me - ru - e -
- go, cu - jus vi - sce-ra me - ru - e -
- go, cu - jus vi - sce-ra me - ru - e -

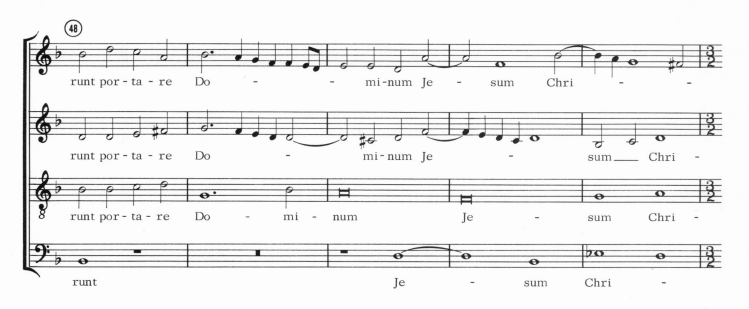

runt por-ta-re Do - - mi-num Je - sum Chri - -
runt por-ta-re Do - - mi-num Je - sum Chri -
runt por-ta-re Do - mi - num Je - sum Chri -
runt Je - sum Chri -

stum. Al - le - lu - ia, Al - le - lu - ia, Al - le - lu -
stum. Al - le - lu - ia, Al - le - lu - ia, Al - le - lu -
stum. Al - le - lu - ia, Al - le - lu - ia, Al - le - lu -
stum. Al - le - lu -

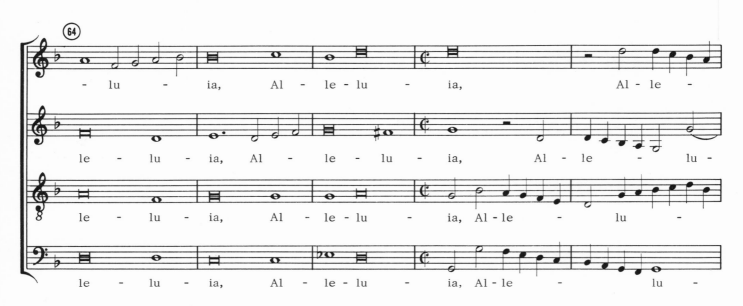

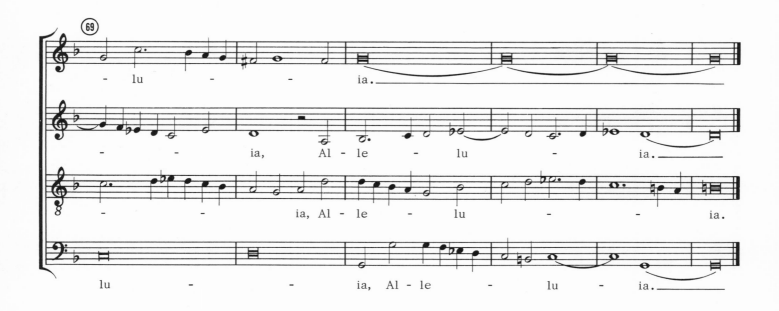

KYRIE ELEISON

from *Missa: O Magnum Mysterium*

Victoria

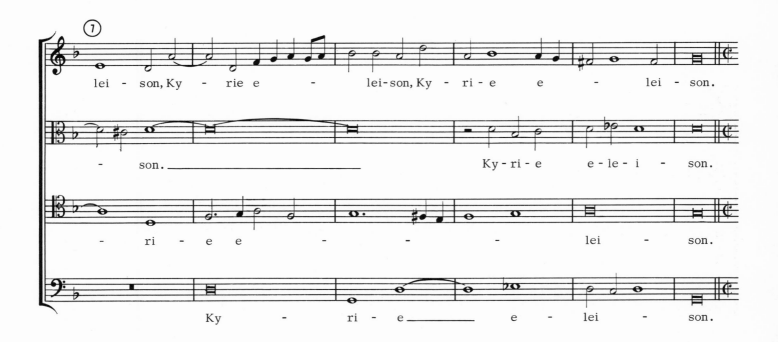

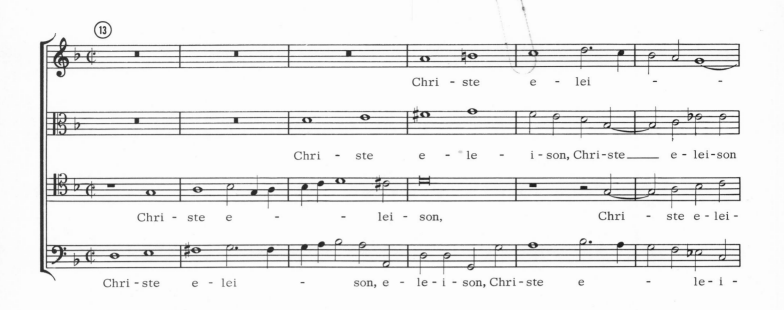

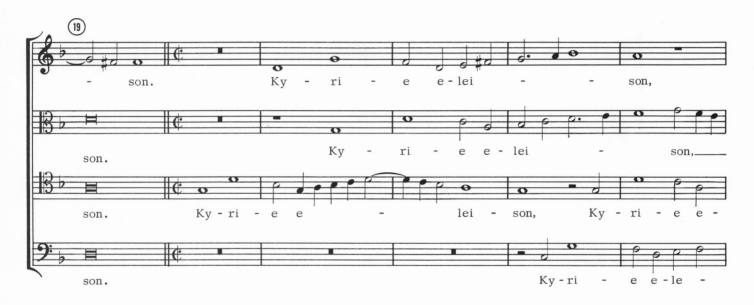

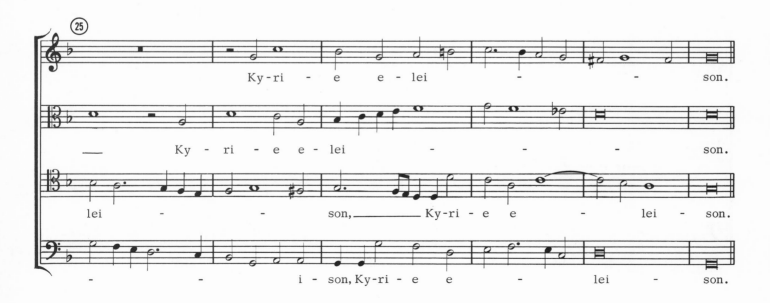

Chanson: MILLE REGRETZ

Josquin des Prez

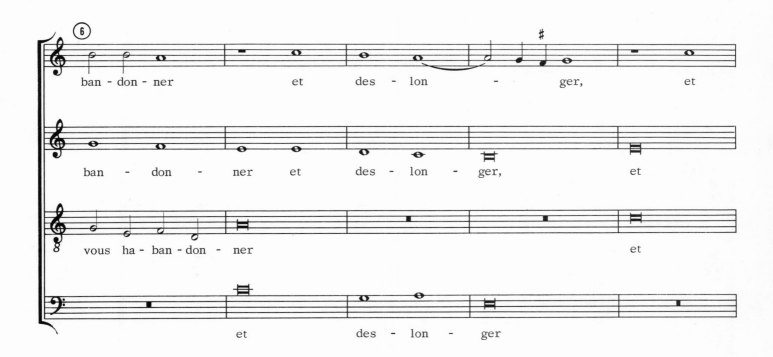

From *Werke van Josquin des Prez*, Vol. 8
Copyright 1925 by G. Alsbach & Co., Amsterdam. Reprinted by permission.

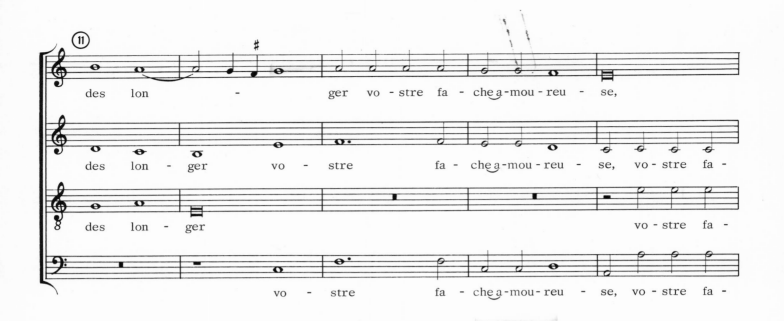

des lon - ger vo - stre fa - che a - mou - reu - se,

des lon - ger vo - stre fa - che a - mou - reu - se, vo - stre fa -

des lon - ger vo - stre fa -

vo - stre fa - che a - mou - reu - se, vo - stre fa -

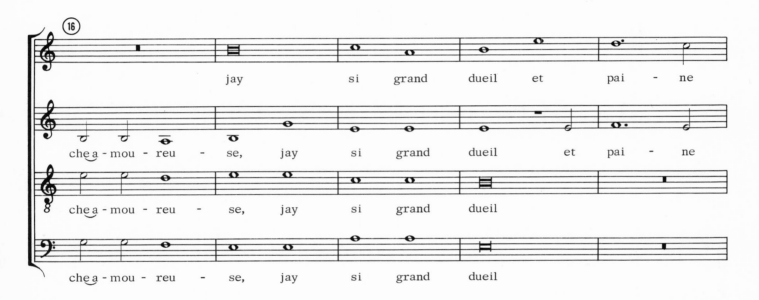

jay si grand dueil et pai - ne

che a - mou - reu - se, jay si grand dueil et pai - ne

che a - mou - reu - se, jay si grand dueil

che a - mou - reu - se, jay si grand dueil

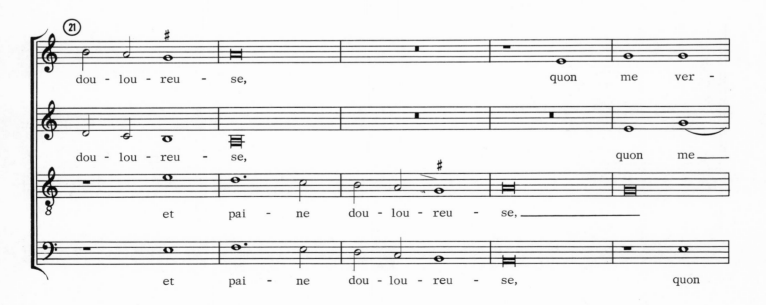

dou - lou - reu - se, quon me ver -

dou - lou - reu - se, quon me

et pai - ne dou - lou - reu - se,

et pai - ne dou - lou - reu - se, quon

228

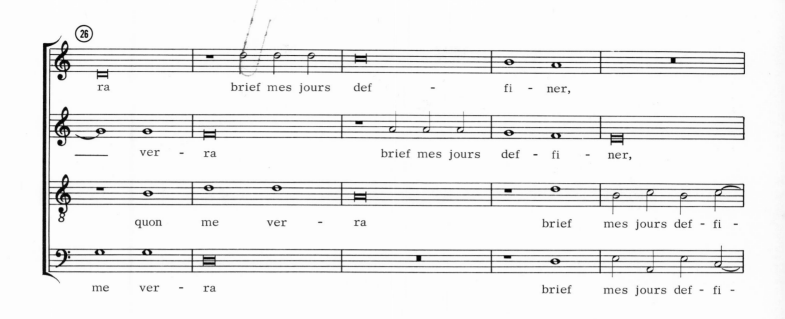

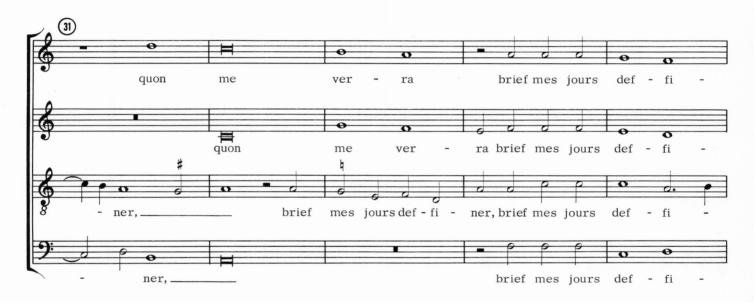

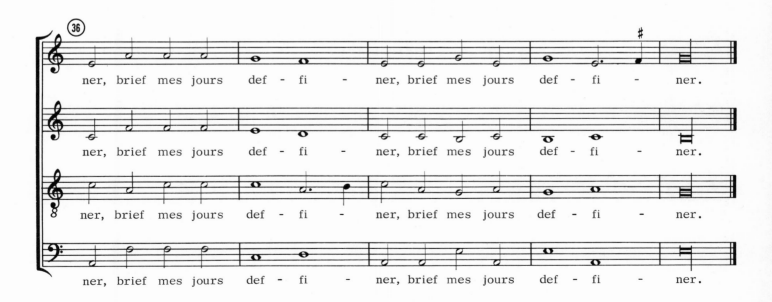

Madrigal: IO MI RIVOLGO INDIETRO

Arcadelt

From *Van Ockeghem tot Sweelinck*, Vol. VII, Dr. A. Smijers, ed.
Copyright 1956 by G. Alsbach & Co., Amsterdam. Reprinted by permission.

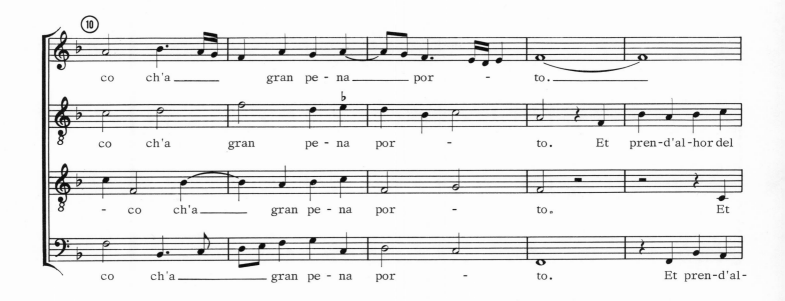

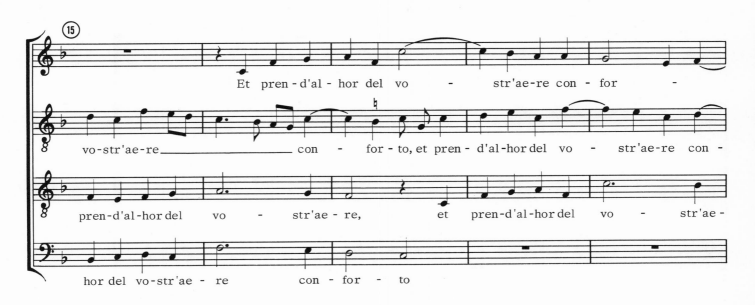

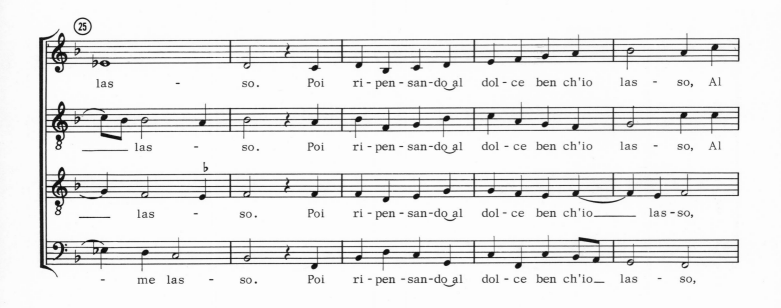

las - so. Poi ri - pen - san - do al dol - ce ben ch'io las - so, Al

las - so. Poi ri - pen - san - do al dol - ce ben ch'io las - so, Al

las - so. Poi ri - pen - san - do al dol - ce ben ch'io _____ las - so,

- me las - so. Poi ri - pen - san - do al dol - ce ben ch'io _____ las - so,

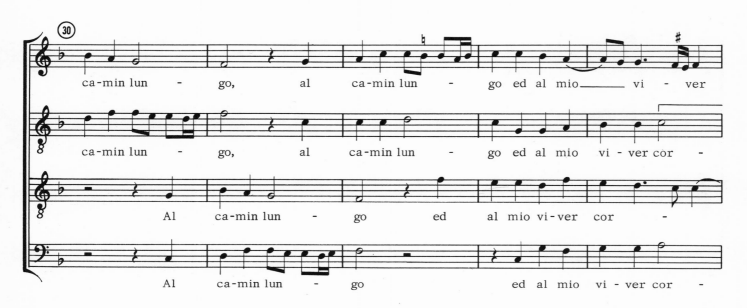

ca - min lun - go, al ca - min lun - go ed al mio _____ vi - ver

ca - min lun - go, al ca - min lun - go ed al mio vi - ver cor -

Al ca - min lun - go ed al mio vi - ver cor -

Al ca - min lun - go ed al mio vi - ver cor -

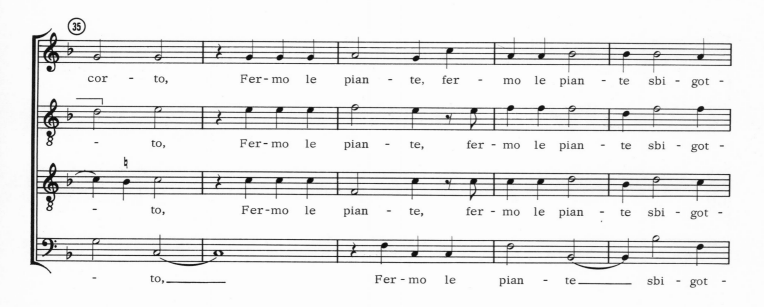

cor - to, Fer - mo le pian - te, fer - mo le pian - te sbi - got -

- to, Fer - mo le pian - te, fer - mo le pian - te sbi - got -

- to, Fer - mo le pian - te, fer - mo le pian - te sbi - got -

- to, _____ Fer - mo le pian - te _____ sbi - got -

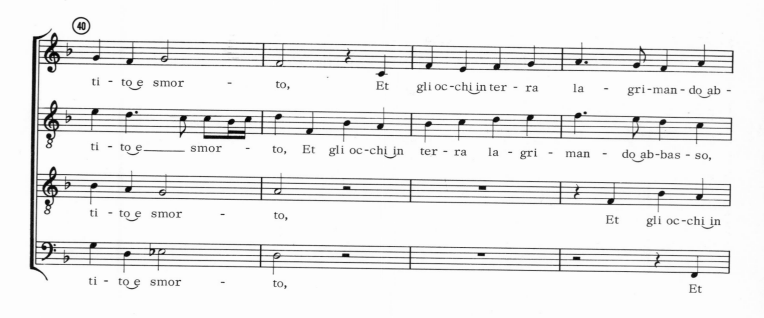

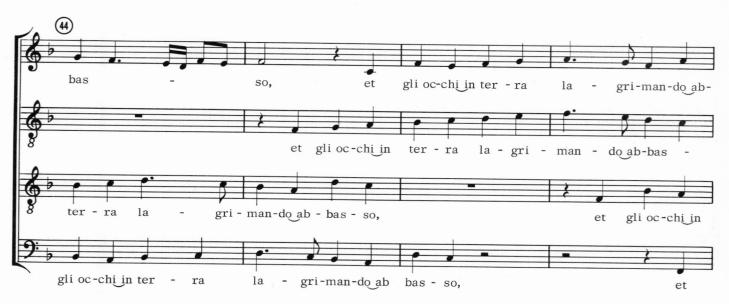

Madrigal: SE NEL PARTIR DA VOI

Monteverdi

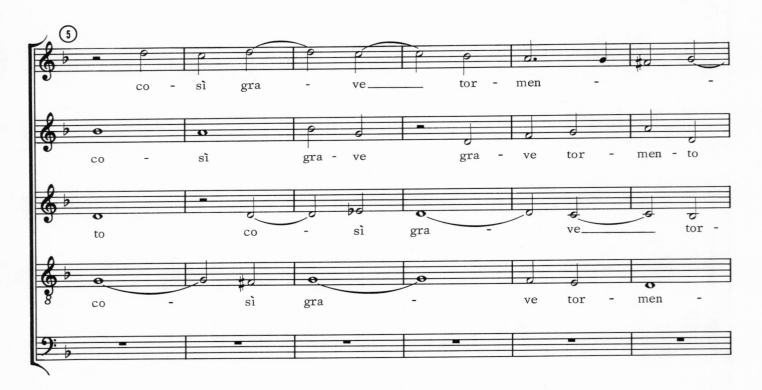

From *Tutte le Opere di Monteverdi*, Vol. I
Copyright 1942 by The Mediaeval Academy of America, Cambridge, Mass. Used by permission.

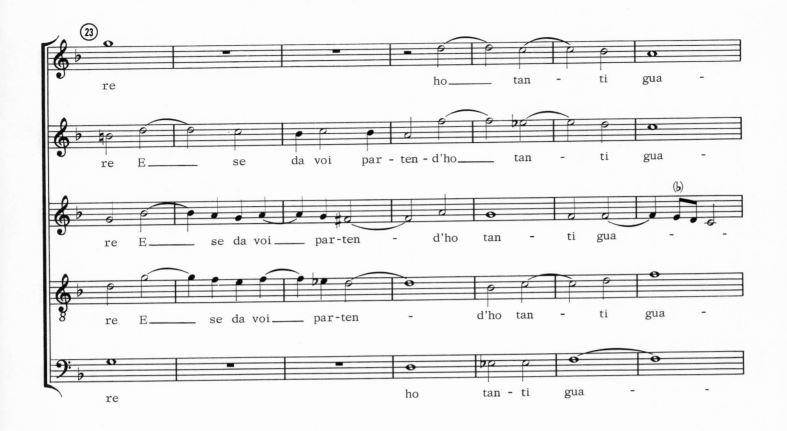

re

re E_____ se da voi par-ten-d'ho_____ tan - ti gua -

re E_____ se da voi_____ par-ten - d'ho tan - ti gua -

re E_____ se da voi_____ par-ten - d'ho tan - ti gua -

re ho tan - ti gua -

i Pos-s'io pri - ma mo - rir Pos-s'io pri - ma mo - rir

i Pos-s'io pri - ma mo - rir

i che par-tir ma - i che par-tir ma -

i_____ che par-tir ma - i che

i Pos-s'io pri - ma mo - rir che par-tir

236

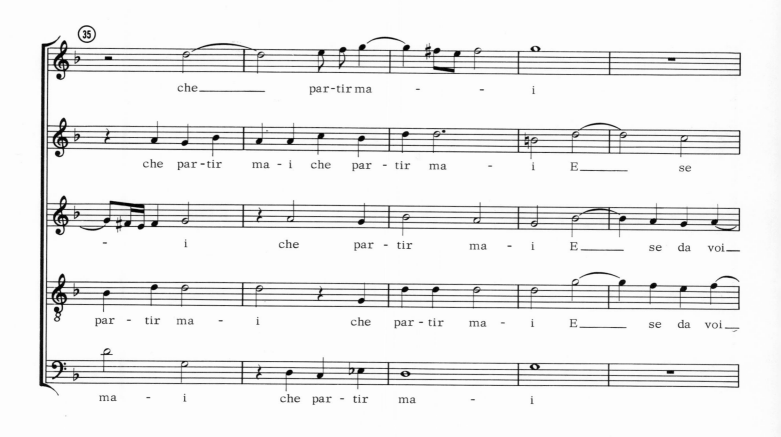

che_____ par-tir ma \- i

che par-tir ma - i che par - tir ma - i E_____ se

\- i che par-tir ma - i E____ se da voi___

par - tir ma - i che par-tir ma - i E_____ se da voi___

ma - i che par-tir ma - i

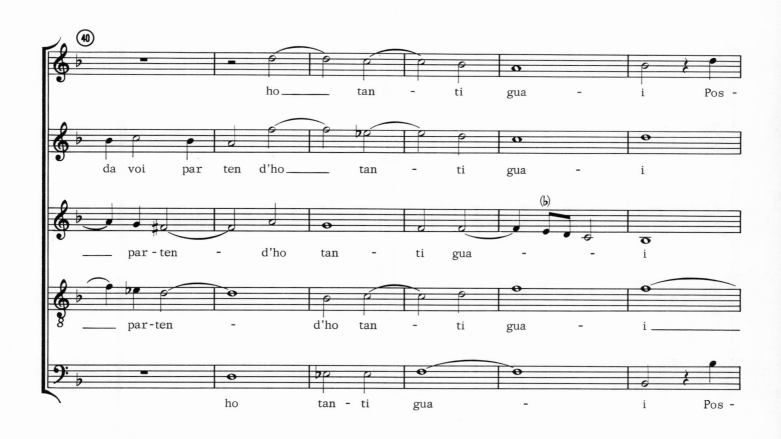

ho_____ tan - ti gua - i Pos-

da voi par ten d'ho_____ tan - ti gua - i

____ par-ten - d'ho tan - ti gua - i

____ par-ten - d'ho tan - ti gua - i_____

ho tan - ti gua - i Pos-

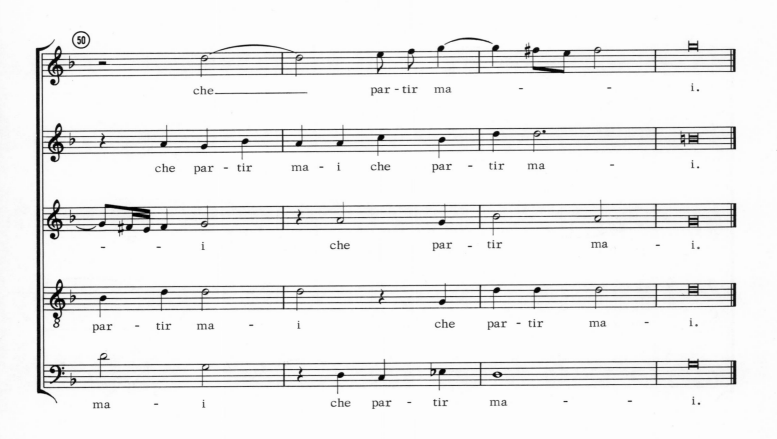

Madrigal: RESTA DI DARMI NOIA

Gesualdo

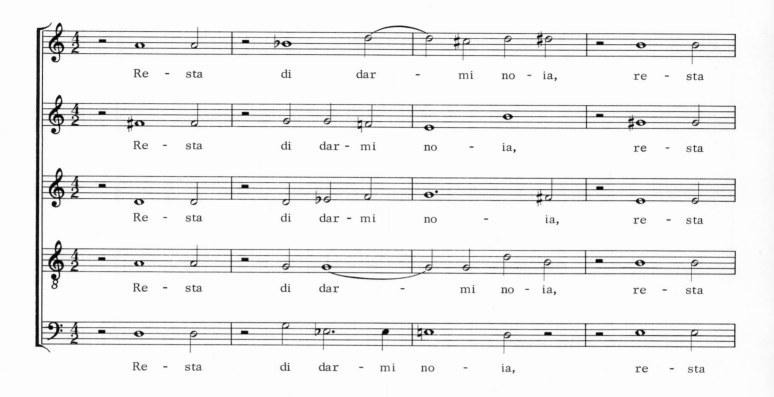

Re - sta di dar - mi no - ia, re - sta

Re - sta di dar - mi no - ia, re - sta

Re - sta di dar - mi no - ia, re - sta

Re - sta di dar - mi no - ia, re - sta

Re - sta di dar - mi no - ia, re - sta

di dar - mi no - ia, pen - sier cru - do e fal - la -

di dar - mi no - ia, pen - sier cru - do e fal - la -

di dar - mi no - ia, pen - sier cru - do e fal - la -

di dar - mi no - ia, pen - sier cru - do e fal - la -

di dar - mi no - ia, pen - sier cru - do e fa -

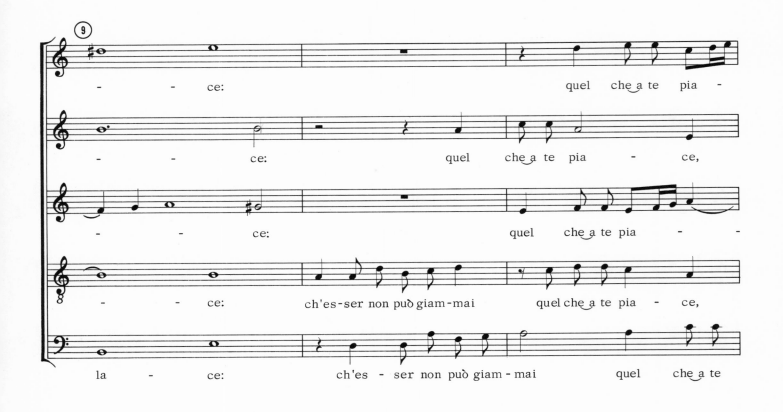

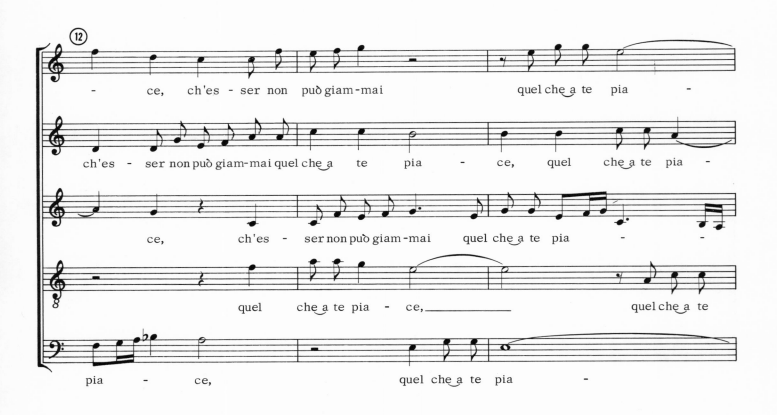

240

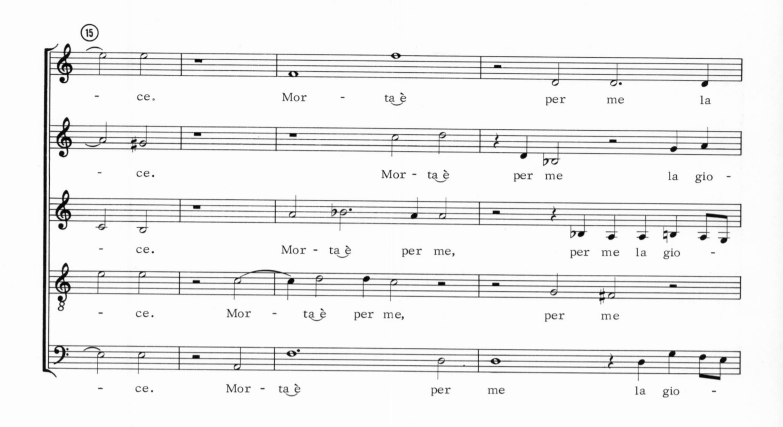

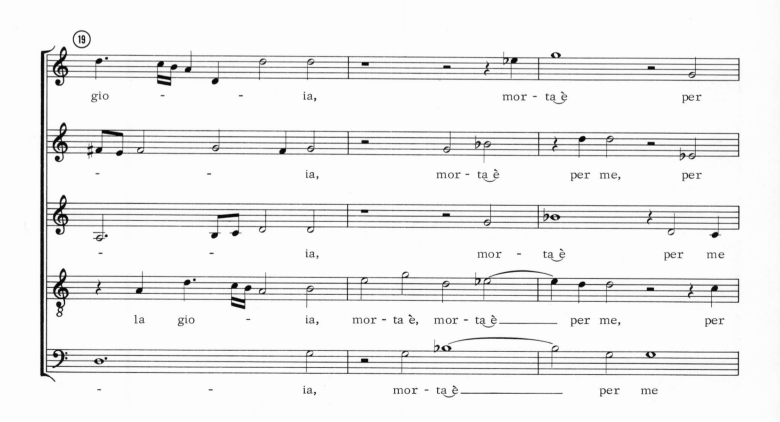

me la gio - - ia, spe-rar

me la gio - - ia, on de spe-rar, spe-rar non li -

la gio - - ia, on - de spe-rar, spe-rar non

me la gio - ia, on - de spe-rar, spe-rar

la gio - - ia, on - de spe-rar,___ spe-rar non

non li - ce d'es - ser mai più, mai più fe - li - ce.

ce, non li - ce d'es - ser mai più, mai più fe - li - ce.

li - ce, non li - ce d'es - ser mai più, mai più fe - li - ce.

non li - ce d'es - ser mai più, mai più fe - li - ce.

li - ce d'es - ser mai più, mai più fe - li - ce.

RICERCARE

Cavazzoni

GALLIARD

Byrd

FANTASIA

Tomkins

Permission for reprint granted by Stainer & Bell, Ltd., London; Galaxy Music Corporation, New York, agents.

247

UNIT V

POLYPHONY FROM THE NINTH CENTURY

TO THE FIFTEENTH CENTURY

A. Sing and/or play the work. What observations do you have to make about sonority, texture, and spacing?

B. Analyze each line.
1. Rhythm (use of metric patterns, rhythmic modes, etc.)
2. Shape of the line
3. Establishment of mode
4. Predominant melodic intervals
5. Points of rest (rhythmic and melodic treatment)

C. Study the relationship between the parts.
1. Identification of each harmonic interval
2. Characteristic cadence formulas
3. Rhythmic variety
4. Elements of tension and relaxation
5. Compositional devices

D. Discuss other features.
1. Meter and tempo
2. Texture
3. Text setting*
4. Form

E. Compare the work to others in this unit and to works of other periods.

*Translations appear on pages 321-322, 325-327.

Composite Organum at the Fifth: SIT GLORIA DOMINI

from *Musica Enchiriadis*

9th Century

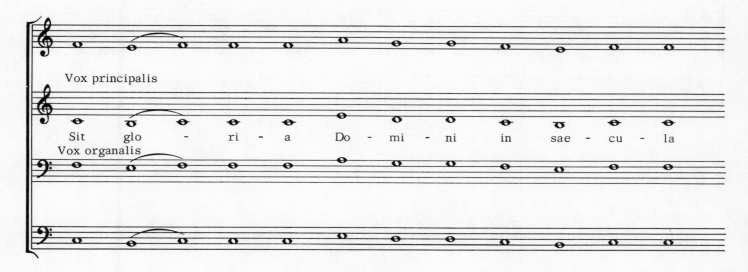

Vox principalis

Sit glo - ri - a Do - mi - ni in sae - cu - la

Vox organalis

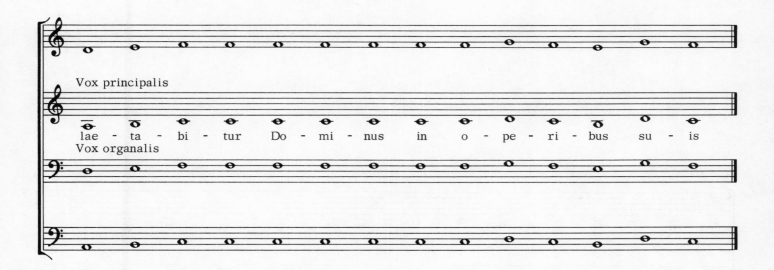

Vox principalis

lae - ta - bi - tur Do - mi - nus in o - pe - ri - bus su - is

Vox organalis

Excerpt from MIRA LEGE, MIRO MODO

12th Century

Mi - ra le - ge, mi - ro mo - do, De - us for - mat __ ho - mi - nem

Mi - ra ma - gis hunc re - for - mat __ vi - de mi - rum or - di - nem.

Melismatic Organum: CUNCTIPOTENS GENITOR

School of Compostela (c. 1125)

Cun - cti - po - tens ge - ni - tor,

De - us om - ni - cre - a - tor,

e - ley - son.

Cri - ste, De - i for - ma,

vir - tus pa - tris - que so - phi - a,

e - ley - son. Am - bo - rum sa - crum

spi - ra - men ne - xus a - mor - que, e - ley - son.

Hymn (in Conductus Style): NATO NOBIS HODIE

13th Century

Na - to no - bis ho - di - e   de Ma - ri - a   vir - gi - ne

e - ter - no re - gi glo - ri - ae   cum su - a - vi

iu - bi - lo De - o di - ca - mus gra - ti - as.

Motet: O MITISSIMA (QUANT VOI)—VIRGO—HEC DIES

13th Century

*Note that the top voice may sing either the Latin or French text.

lon,   A - donc pleur et sou - pir

xi - li - um   Det   et re - me - di - um

Do - mi - num,   Per te, Ma - ri - a,

es   Hec

Pour le grant de - sir   Qu'ai de la bel - le

Con - tra de - mo - num   Fal - li - bi - les   as -

De - tur ve - ni - a,   An - ge - lo nun -

di - -

Ma - ri - on,   Qui mon cuer a en pri - son.

tu - ci - as   Et ho - rum ne - qui - ci - as.

ci - an - te,   Vir - go es post et an - te.

- - - - es

KYRIE II

from *La Messe de Nostre Dame*

Machaut

Caccia: SEGUGI A CORDE

Magister Piero

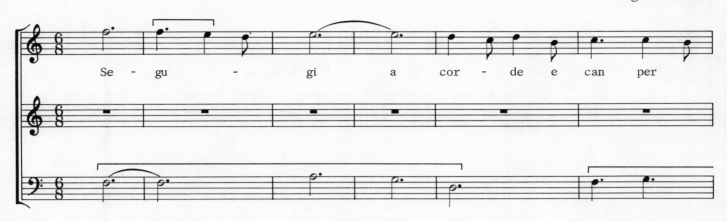

la, ol - la ol - la!" "Qual è, qual è, qual è, vien quà, vien
tan - do, "Ve' la, ve' la, ve'!" "Dra-gon, dra-gon, te,

quà, che quì son gli or - si!" Di - ce - va
te!" "Ol - la, ol - la, ol - la "Qual è, qual è, qual è, vien quà, vien

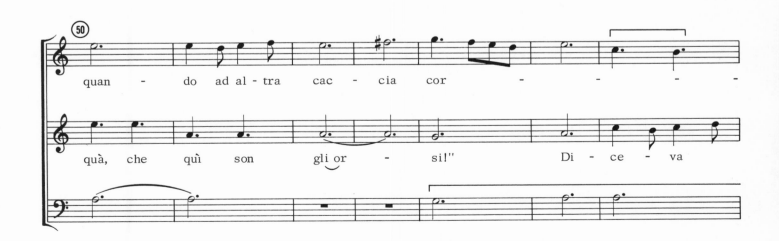

quan - do ad al - tra cac - cia cor - - - -
quà, che quì son gli or - si!" Di - ce - va

si.

quan - do ad al - tra cac - cia cor - si.

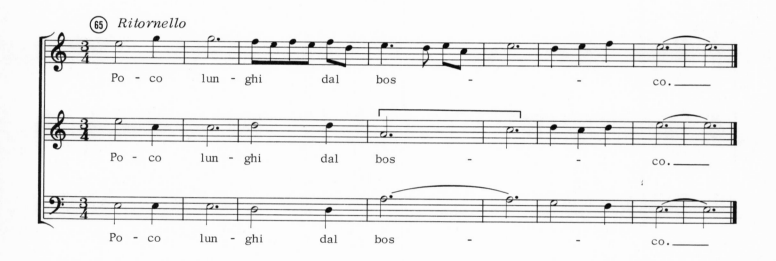

Po - co lun - ghi dal bos - - co.____

Po - co lun - ghi dal bos - - co.____

Po - co lun - ghi dal bos - - co.____

Al suon de' corni e de l'altra tempesta,
D'una vallea uscì la villanella.
"Ai, ai, ai, da', da', a la Volpe!"
Allor la presi per la man, "Vien qua,
Quà, lascia andar la volpe!"
Disse, "De no, de no, perchè i' non voglio!"
Pur l'abbracciai che non le valse orgoglio;
E porta la nel bosco.

KYRIE ELEISON

from *Missa: Sancti Jacobi*

Dufay

Ky - ri - e

Ky - - ri - e

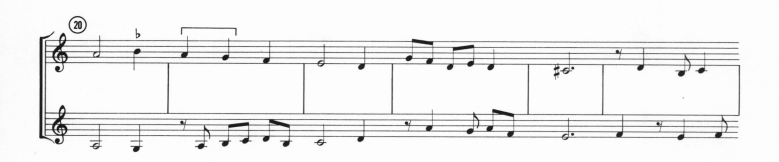

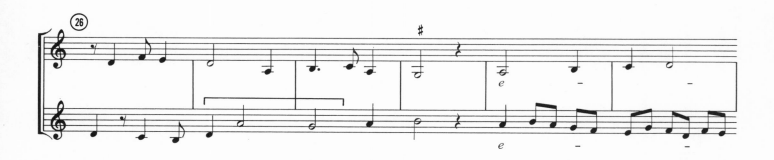

e - -

e - -

- - - - lei - son.

- - - - lei - son.

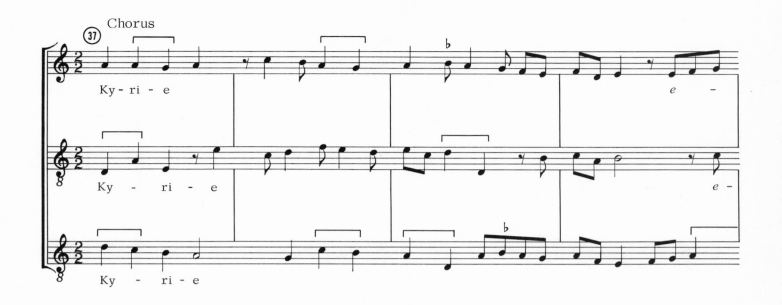

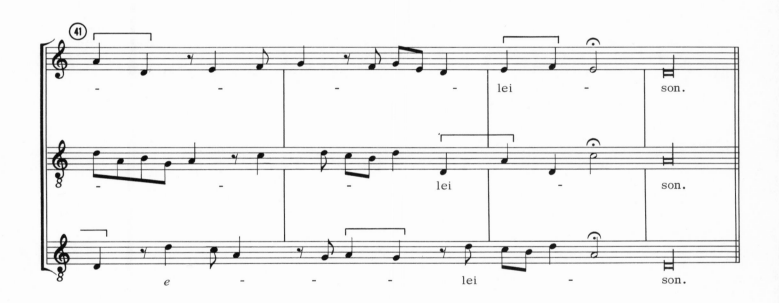

OSANNA

from *Missa: Prolationum*

Ockeghem

UNIT VI

POLYPHONY FROM THE EIGHTEENTH AND NINETEENTH CENTURIES

A. Perform the music.

B. Study the melodic material of the work.
   1. Rhythm and shape
   2. Implied harmonies
   3. Statements and recurrences of principle and subordinate melodic ideas

C. Outline the formal structure.
   1. Grouping into large sections
   2. Connecting material (episodes, etc.)
   3. Key relationships
   4. Balance and proportion
   5. Comparative study of recurring sections

D. Analyze the work harmonically.
   1. Harmonic functions
   2. Nonharmonic tones
   3. Modulations
   4. Cadential structures
   5. Harmonic rhythm
   6. Use of chromaticism

E. Discuss the developmental features.
   1. Compositional devices
   2. Texture
   3. Tension and relaxation
   4. High points
   5. Metric and rhythmic shifts

F. Compare the work to others in this unit and to works of other periods.

*Translation of the Brahms text appears on page 327.

A LITTLE GIGUE FOR PIANO

Mozart, K. 574

274

FUGUE IN G MINOR

Mozart, K. 401

276

280

QUARTET IN C♯ MINOR

(First Movement)

Beethoven, Op. 131

Adagio, ma non troppo e molto espressivo

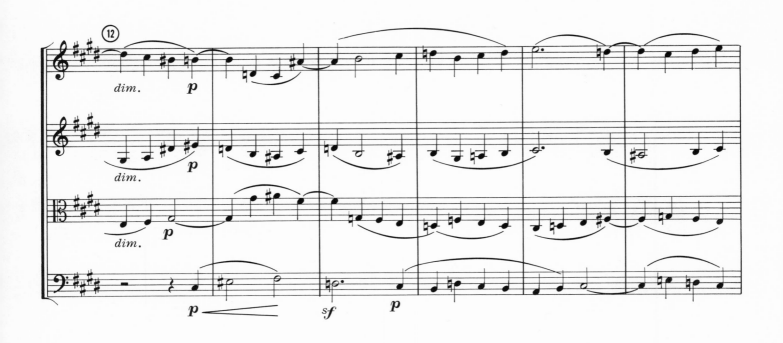

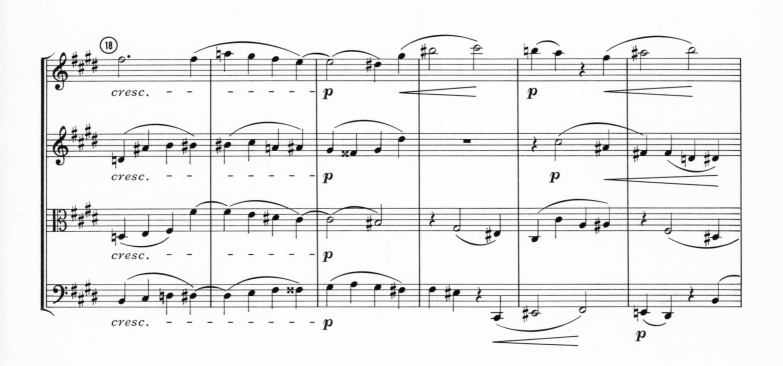

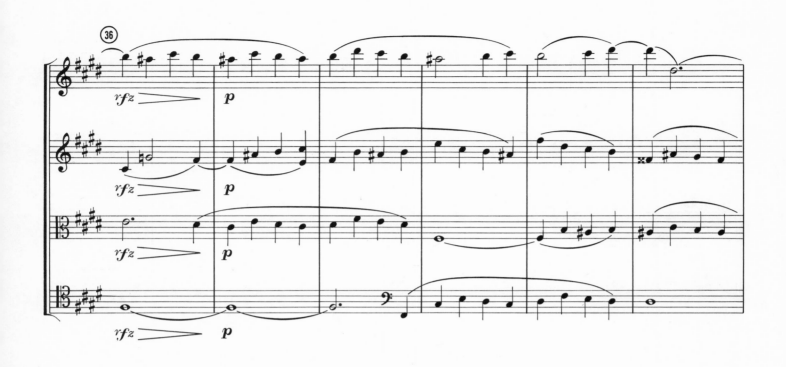

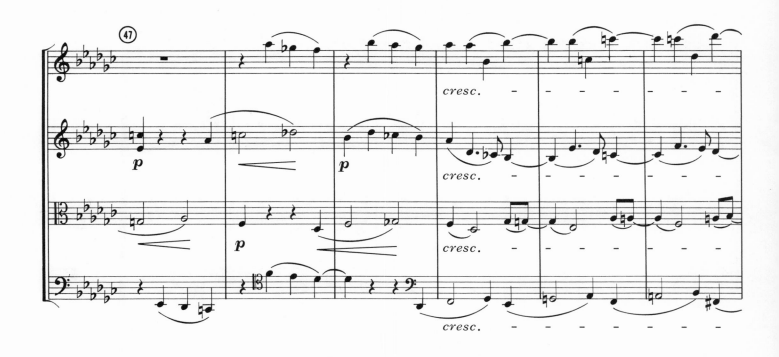

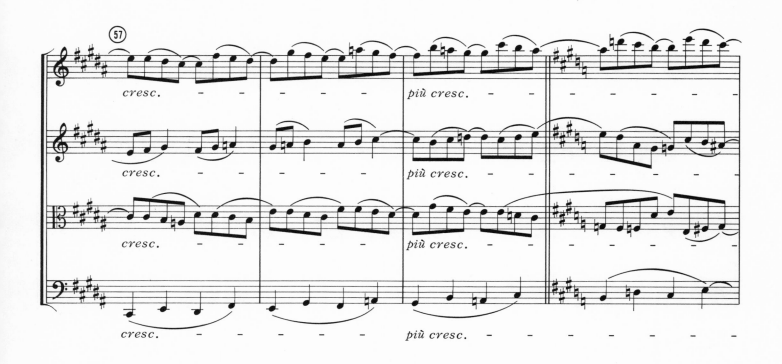

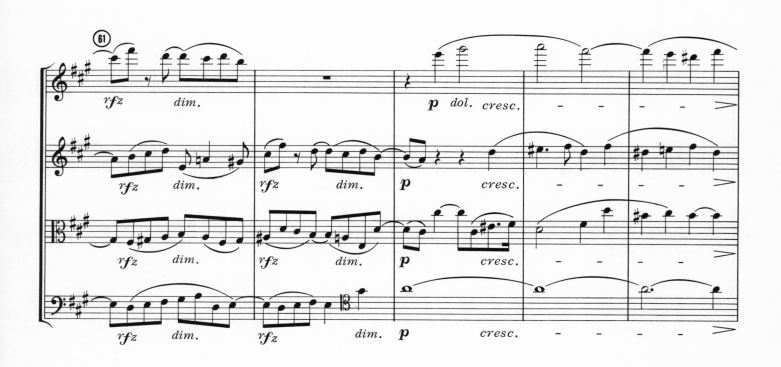

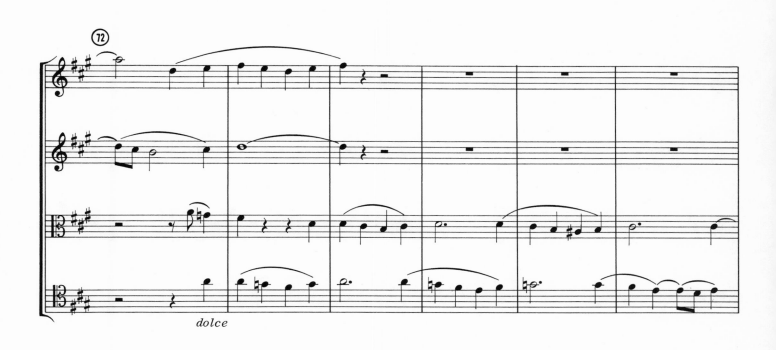

dolce

287

288

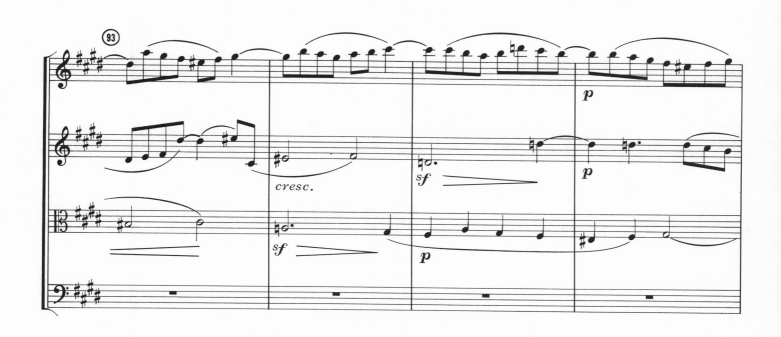

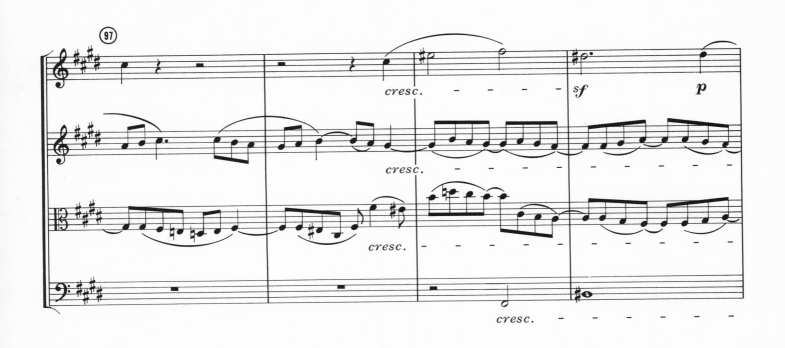

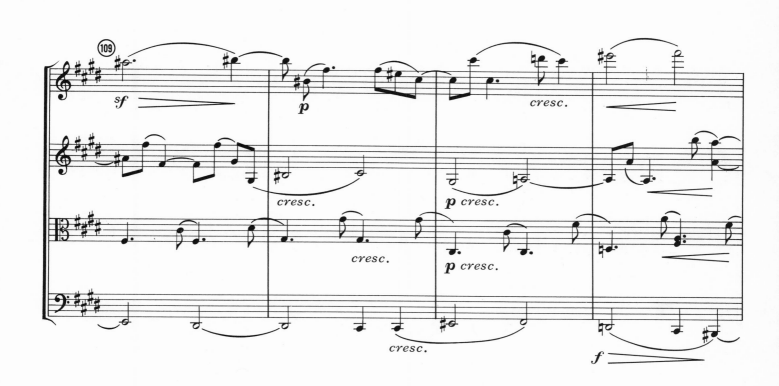

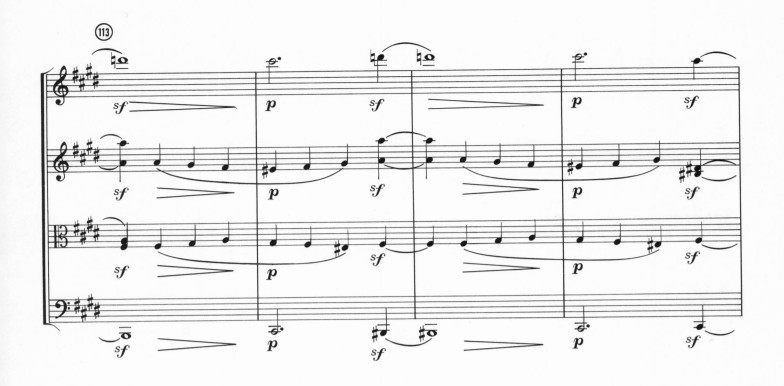

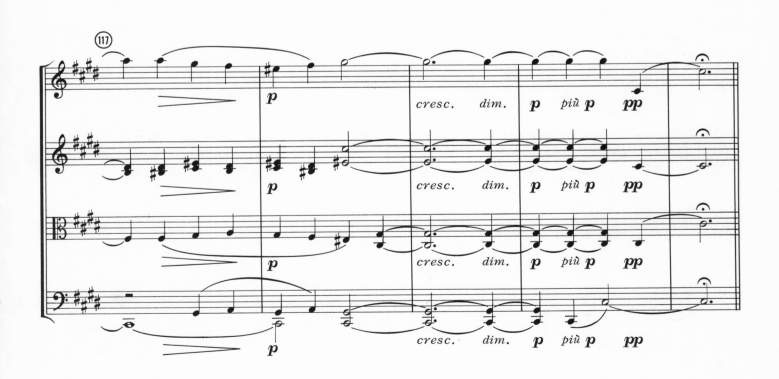

Chorale Prelude: O WIE SELIG SEID IHR DOCH, IHR FROMMEN

Brahms, Op. 122, No. 6

Gott ge - kom - men!

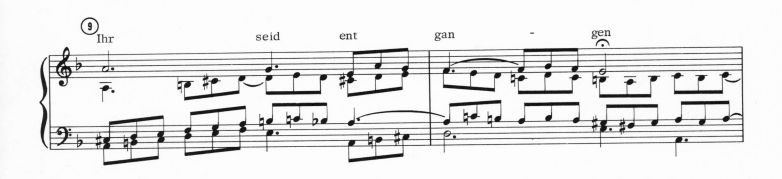

Ihr seid ent - gan - gen

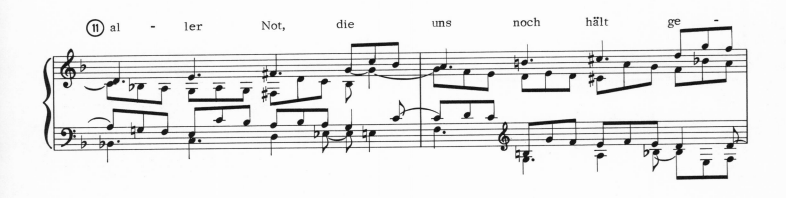

al - ler Not, die uns noch hält ge -

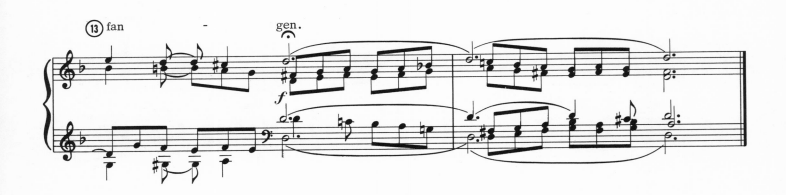

fan - gen.

CANON IN D MINOR

Reger

Moderato

UNIT VII

POLYPHONY FROM THE TWENTIETH CENTURY

SUGGESTIONS AND QUESTIONS FOR ANALYSIS AND DISCUSSION

A. Discuss the organization of the work.
1. Is there a basic tonal center?
2. Is it based on a tone row?
3. What is the formal structure?

B. Prepare a melodic and rhythmic analysis of the work.
What is there that is characteristic of the 20th century?

C. Study the harmonies.
1. What intervals are featured? Where do they occur rhythmically (on the strong beat, off the beat, etc.)?
2. What kinds of chord structures are used?
3. Analyze the cadences.
4. Are there chord progressions in the traditional sense?
5. What determines the composers' choice of the harmonies?

D. Point out the developmental features of the work.
1. How are motives treated?
2. What compositional devices are used?
3. Where do contrasting sections occur?
4. What elements create tension or relaxation?
5. Where are the high points?
6. If this is a serial composition, how does the composer manipulate his basic set?

E. Discuss other significant aspects which should be considered in order to perform the work intelligently.

F. Compare the work with others of similar nature in this and other units of the book.

*Text translation of the Stravinsky excerpt appears on page 327.

CHROMATIC INVENTION

from *Mikrokosmos, Vol. III*

Bartók (1935)

[55 sec.]

FUGUE IN F

from *Ludus Tonalis*

Hindemith (1943)

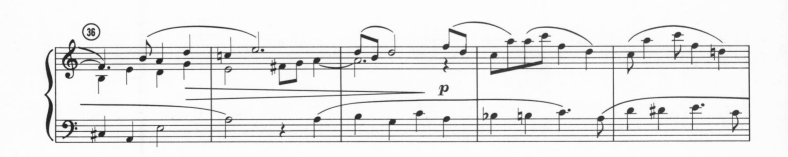

Excerpt from FUGUE III

from *String Quartet No. 3*

Harris (1939)

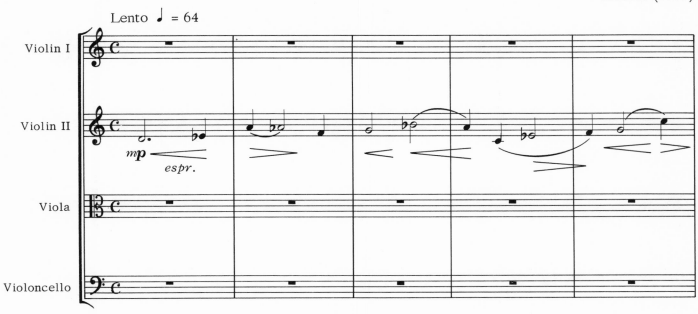

305

SYMPHONY OF PSALMS

(Excerpt from Second Movement)

Stravinsky (1930)

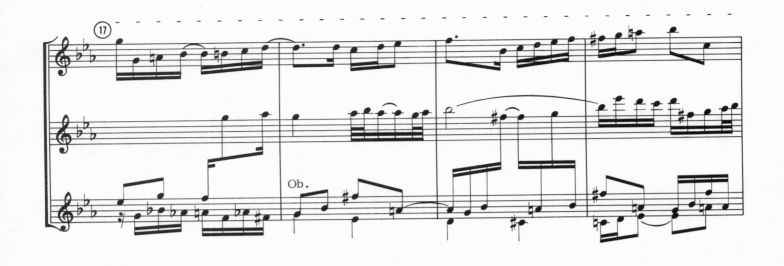

mi - - se-ri ae,___ et___ de-la-to-fae - cis.

me - as; et e - du - xit me da la - cu mi - se - ri - ae.

___ et in - ten - dit, et in-ten-dit mi - hi Et

Ex - pec - tans ex-pec - ta - vi Do-mi-num, et

Fl.

Tbn.

VARIATION II

from *Variations for Piano*

Webern, Op. 27

APPENDIX

DEFINITIONS

CACCIA   A 14th-century form, generally for two voices (in canon) and one instrumental part. The text, as the name suggests, often deals with a hunting scene. (ex. p. 263)

CADENCE A melodic or harmonic point of rest. Some examples follow:

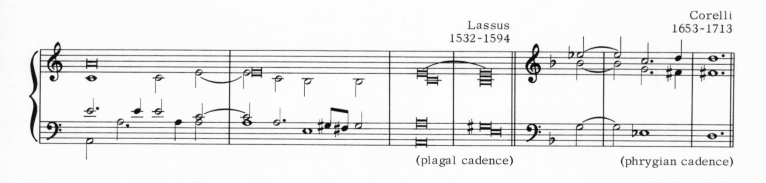

J. S. Bach
1685-1750

(deceptive cadence)   (authentic cadence)

Hindemith, *Ludus Tonalis*, Fugue in E

© 1920 by Universal Edition Renewed 1948. Copyright and Renewal
assigned to Boosey and Hawkes, Inc. Reprinted by permission.

Bartók, *Studies*, Op. 18

CANON   Composition for two or more voices using strict imitation. In analyzing a canon, the following elements should be noted: number of voices, interval of imitation (at the 8ve, the 5th, etc.), time elapsed between entrance of each voice (after two measures, after three beats, etc.), compositional device used (in augmentation, in inversion, etc.). (ex. pp. 37, 39)

In an *enigma* canon, the composer withholds some of the information pertaining to the structure, leaving the solution to the student or performer. (ex. p. 116)

CANTATA A liturgical or secular vocal work of several movements. Generally, there are movements for chorus and recitatives, arias, and duets for soloists. The liturgical cantata frequently ends with a harmonized chorale. In the chorale cantata, the chorale melody may act as a *cantus firmus* in some or all of the movements. (ex. p. 162-166)

CANTUS FIRMUS

A melodic line, often in long note values, which serves as a basis around which other lines are woven in counterpoint. The cantus firmus may be a portion of a chant, a chorale tune, popular melody, etc. (ex. pp. 257, 185)

CHORALE PRELUDE

A polyphonic work, usually for organ, that is based on a chorale melody. (ex. pp. 61-73)

CHORALE VARIATIONS (Chorale Partita)

A set of variations based on a chorale melody.   Occasionally one may find the variations set in the form of a suite. (ex. pp. 59-60)

COMPOSITIONAL DEVICE

Repetition of a musical idea through which a composer may achieve unity in a composition. References to typical examples are listed below.

exact repetition - in most binary dance forms each part repeats. (ex. p. 5 m. 1-8)

imitation - (ex. p. 3 m. 1-4)

sequence - (ex. p. 24 m. 3-5, 9-11, m. 14-17)

melodic inversion - (ex. p. 133 m. 20-23: alto, the subject is inverted)

retrograde - (ex. pp. 300-302: m. 30-59 are retrograde of m. 1-30)

augmentation - (ex. p. 144: in m. 2-6, the upper voice has an augmentation in inversion of the subject)

fragmentation - (ex. pp. 282-283: in m. 20-24, fragments of the subject are used in sequence and imitation in the outer voices)

CONCERTO GROSSO

A work of several movements for a small group of instrumentalists (*concertino*) and orchestra (*ripieno* or *tutti*).   The contrast of textures between the lighter *concertino* and the heavier *ripieno* is significant in the concerti of Corelli, Vivaldi, Handel, Bach, and others. (ex. p. 174) The quick movements are often in ritornello form.

In the *solo concerto*, a single instrument is contrasted with the orchestral group. Many solo keyboard works exist in which concerto-like contrasts play a significant role (see the Prelude to Bach's *English Suite No. 3* and his *Italian Concerto*).

CONDUCTUS

A 12th- or 13th-century work in Latin for one, two, or three voices. The melodic lines are freely composed (not based on Gregorian chant). The setting is usually in note-against-note style. (ex. p. 258)

FANTASIA

In the Baroque era, a work that is in a free, improvisatory style. In the 16th and 17th centuries, it was in the learned or fugal style similar to that of an instrumental motet or ricercar. (ex. pp. 247, 243)

FUGUE   A highly developed contrapuntal instrumental or vocal work (usually for three or four voices) which is based primarily on a melodic idea (the *subject*) that is introduced at the beginning.   The subject is immediately imitated by a second voice (the *answer*) while the first continues in counterpoint.   The other voices also enter in order, stating the subject and answer.   The fugue is extended through a series of *episodes* (often in double or triple counterpoint) which modulate to related keys and statements of the subject (or answer) in the new keys.   The original key reappears at the close of the fugue.   Some of the terms used in analysis of fugue are:

   exposition - the first portion of the fugue where entries of subject and answer appear in the tonic and dominant keys. (ex. p. 125: m. 1-9)

   real answer - an exact transposition of the subject. (ex. p. 132: m. 5-8)

   tonal answer - an intervallic adjustment is made in the imitation. The answer therefore is not an exact transposition of the subject. (ex. p. 125: m. 3-4)

   countersubject - counterpoint that appears in a consistent manner when the subject is stated (consequently the countersubject and the subject are in double counterpoint). (ex. p. 128: m. 3-4 etc.)

   stretto - a canonic section based on the subject.   The second voice enters before the first voice has completed its statement. (ex. p 138 m: 19-21)

   In some fugues, the subject appears in *inversion, augmentation*, etc. (ex. p. 144)

   A *double fugue* is based on two subjects which may be introduced simultaneously at the beginning or may be developed independently (that is, in separate expositions) before combining. (ex. p. 151)

   An *Invention* is a short, fugue-like composition for two or three voices. The first imitation, however, is frequently at the octave. (ex. p. 22)

   The *Ricercar(e)* and the *Canzona* are instrumental works which were forerunners of the fugue. (ex. pp. 243, 121)

INVERTIBLE COUNTERPOINT

Counterpoint written in such a manner that the voices may exchange places and still maintain acceptable harmonic relationships. In the following example:

(6   3   2   3   4   6)

the upper voice may be transposed down an octave:

(3   6   7   6   5   3)

(double counterpoint at the octave). This technique may involve more than two voices (triple counterpoint, quadruple counterpoint, etc.). Other intervals of transposition (at the 10th, 12th, and 15th) may be used. A device of the 13th century in which voices exchange parts without transposition is called *stimmtausch*.

MADRIGAL

A secular vocal work. In the 16th century the madrigal was an amorous poem set for three to six (usually five) voice-parts. The texture employs imitative techniques with occasional sections in "familiar style" (chordal style). Significant words are often highlighted by chromaticism, melismas, and other coloristic effects. (ex. pp. 230, 234, 239)

The *frottola* is a forerunner of the madrigal. (ex. p. 197)

MASS

The most significant formal rite of the Catholic Church. The *Proper* is that portion of the mass which varies with each service. That part of the mass which does not change from day to day is known as the *Ordinary* and is the portion which is generally set by composers. The normal order of movements in the composed mass is: *Kyrie*, *Gloria*, *Credo*, *Sanctus*, and *Agnus Dei*. A translation of the text of the *Ordinary* appears on pp. 321, 322.

MODES (CHURCH MODES, ECCLESIASTIC MODES, MEDIEVAL MODES)

Scale formations in use in the Middle Ages and following centuries:

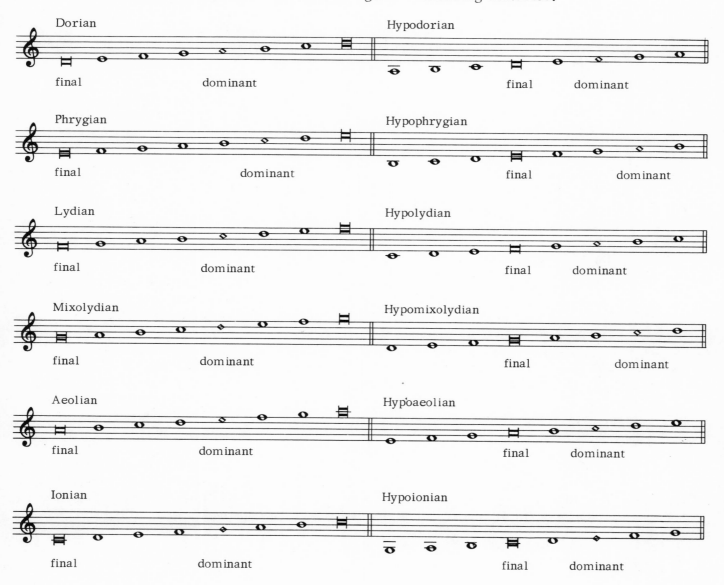

MOTET   In 16th-century Renaissance music, a sacred vocal work for four or more voice-parts. The work is often set in an imitative manner with great variety of rhythm and texture. (ex. pp. 192, 220)

    In the 13th and 14th centuries, the motet had a tenor line which was based on a portion of a Gregorian Chant. This was set in long note values, often in isorhythm. A second (and at times a third) voice, with a different text often in another language, was added to the cantus firmus. (ex. p. 259)

MUSICA FICTA

In modal music, the use of certain chromatic tones. "Bb" frequently occurs to correct for the tritone and in descending melodic lines. In 16th-century music, F♯, C♯, and G♯ are employed as leading tones. The third, if present in final cadence chords, was often raised. (ex. p. 193: m. 6, m. 11, m. 22, m. 24, m. 26, m. 32)

ORATORIO

A large work for chorus, soloists, and orchestra, often based upon a Biblical theme. The text of the oratorio often unfolds chronologically and dramatically, at times in the manner of an opera. Choral movements, solos, duets, etc., are featured.

    The *passion* deals with the events leading up to the crucifixion. (ex. p. 157)

OSTINATO, BASSO OSTINATO, GROUND BASS

A melodic figure most often in the bass, that repeats continuously throughout the course of a section of a composition or throughout an entire movement. The *passacaglia* and the *chaconne* are two variation forms which utilize ostinati. (ex. pp. 43, 92, 89)

PRELUDE   During the Renaissance, a keyboard or lute work in a free and improvisatory style. During the Baroque period, a prelude was written to precede another work, such as a fugue or a suite. The Baroque prelude may be in a form similar to that of a toccata, an invention, a sonata movement, concerto-grosso movement, etc. (ex. pp. 20, 145)

RITORNELLO

In Baroque music, the passage of instrumental music that introduces an aria or concerto grosso and recurs in different keys through the body of the piece. (ex. p. 153: m. 1-8, etc.)

    In the 14th century, the final two lines of a madrigal or a caccia.) (ex. p. 266)

SONATA   In the Baroque era, an instrumental work of several contrasting movements. The sonata at that time was written for a solo instrument (keyboard, unaccompanied violin, etc.) or for one or more melodic instruments plus continuo (a low stringed instrument and a keyboard realizing the figured bass). In the sonata da chiesa, movements alternate between slow and fast tempi. The fast movements are often fugal. The sonata da camera is essentially a group of dance movements. (ex. pp. 35, 107)

A collection of dances all in the same key.   A typical order of dances in the late Baroque period was *allemande, courante* (or *corrente*), *sarabande, gigue,* with an optional dance (*gavotte, minuet,* etc.) between the sarabande and gigue.   The suite may begin with a prelude or fantasia.

The dances are usually in Binary form: ‖:a:‖:b:‖ or ‖:a:‖: b a:‖.   The "b" tends to be some kind of motivic elaboration on the "a".   Some of the dances are:

Allemande - $\frac{4}{4}$, moderate tempo, short up-beat, short figures move through the various voices (ex. p. 74)

Corrente - triple time ($\frac{3}{4}$ or $\frac{3}{8}$), fast, short up-beat, continuous running figures (ex. p. 102)

Courante - $\frac{3}{2}$ or $\frac{6}{4}$, not as fast as the corrente, up-beat, subtle shifts of accents (*hemiola*) (ex. p. 76)

Sarabande - triple meter, slow, feminine cadences, sense of weight often on second beat (ex. p. 78)

Gigue - usually $\frac{6}{8}$ or $\frac{6}{4}$, quick tempo, triplet or dotted-rhythm patterns, frequent use of imitation, inversion of motive in second half of the dance often occurs. (ex. pp. 14, 85)

Gavotte - $\frac{4}{4}$ or ₵, moderate tempo, usually has two quarter-note up-beats, phrases end in middle of the measure (ex. pp. 10, 11)

Minuet - $\frac{3}{4}$, moderate tempo, often followed by a second minuet (trio). The first minuet is restated. (ex. p. 80)

Passepied - $\frac{3}{8}$ or $\frac{6}{8}$, quick tempo, use of up-beat, use of 8 (or 16) bar phrases with repeats.

Bourree - $\frac{4}{4}$ or ₵, quicker than Gavotte, use of up-beat. (ex. p. 5)

TEXTURE   A general term which refers to the "thickness" or "thinness" of a sound, the number and kinds of voices sounding, how they are spaced, how they are grouped, and the melodic-rhythmic relationships between the voices. A passage may be said to have a "light," "thin," or "transparent" texture, as opposed to a "heavy" or "thick" texture. Music in which the voices involved are primarily melodic (fugue, invention, motet, etc.) is said to have a *polyphonic* texture. A single, unaccompanied melodic line is *monophonic*. A passage in which the primary texture is chordal (usually, melody and accompaniment) is *homophonic*. When voices alternate, the texture is called *antiphonal* (as if singing back and forth to each other).

TOCCATA   (from the Italian *toccare*, "to touch") A display piece, for organ or harpsichord, containing full chords, arpeggios, and running scale passages often over pedal points. In many toccatas, the rhapsodic sections alternate with fugal sections.

TRANSLATIONS

THE ORDINARY OF THE MASS

Kyrie

Lord, have mercy. *(Repeat twice more.)*
Christ, have mercy. *(Repeat twice more.)*
Lord, have mercy. *(Repeat twice more.)*

Gloria

Priest: Glory to God in the highest.
People: And on earth peace to men of good will.
We praise you. We bless you. We worship you. We glorify you.
We give you thanks for your great glory.
Lord God, heavenly King, God the Father almighty.
Lord Jesus Christ, the only-begotten Son.
Lord God, Lamb of God, Son of the Father.
You, who take away the sins of the world, have mercy on us.
You, who take away the sins of the world, receive our prayer.
You, who sit at the right hand of the Father, have mercy on us.
For you alone are holy.
You alone are Lord.
You alone, O Jesus Christ, are most high,
With the Holy Spirit, in the glory of God the Father. AMEN.

Credo

Priest: I believe in one God.
People: The Father almighty, maker of heaven and earth, and of all things visible
   and invisible.
And I believe in one Lord, Jesus Christ, the only-begotten Son of God.
Born of the Father before all ages.
God of God, Light of Light, true God of true God.
Begotten, not made, of one substance with the Father.
By whom all things were made.
Who for us men and for our salvation came down from heaven.
And he became flesh by the Holy Spirit of the Virgin Mary: and was made man.
He was also crucified for us, suffered under Pontius Pilate, and was buried.
And on the third day he rose again, according to the Scriptures.
He ascended into heaven and sits at the right hand of the Father.
He will come again in glory to judge the living and the dead.
And of his Kingdom there will be no end.
And I believe in the Holy Spirit, the Lord and Giver of life, who proceeds from the
   the Father and the Son.
Who together with the Father and the Son is adored and glorified, and who spoke
   through the prophets.
And one holy, Catholic, and Apostolic Church.
I confess one baptism for the forgiveness of sins.
And I await the resurrection of the dead.
And the life of the world to come. AMEN.

Sanctus

Holy, holy, holy Lord God of hosts.
Heaven and earth are filled with your glory.
Hosanna in the highest.

Benedictus

Blessed is he who comes in the name of the Lord.
Hosanna in the highest.

Agnus Dei

Lamb of God, who take away the sins of the world, have mercy on us.
Lamb of God, who take away the sins of the world, have mercy on us.
Lamb of God, who take away the sins of the world, grant us peace.

Unit I

BUXTEHUDE: *SALVE, PACIS NUNTIA* (p. 41)

Hail, messenger of peace,
Rainbow (Iris) daughter of the sun,
Rainbow (Iris) daughter of the cloud,
Hail, little jewel of the sky, hail.

Unit II

BACH: ARIA FROM CANTATA NO. 21, *ICH HATTE VIEL BEKÜMMERNISS* (p. 153)

"Seufzer, Thränen, Kummer, Noth"

Sighing, weeping, sorrow, care
Anxious yearning, fear of death,
Nag and gnaw my aching heart,
Tear my troubled soul apart.

SCHÜTZ: RECITATIVE AND CHORUS FROM *ST. JOHN'S PASSION* (p. 157)

Wir haben keine König

Evangelist: Pilate saith unto them,
Pilate: Shall I crucify your King?
Evangelist: The chief priests answered,
Chorus of high priests: We have no king but Caesar.

BACH: CHORUS FROM CANTATA NO. 4 *CHRIST LAG IN TODESBANDEN* (p. 162)

Verse II

Oh, Death, none could thee subdue,
Among all our mortal children,
Our sins brought all this to pass,
For there is no health in us.
Therefore came, came death so soon,
With might he has conquered us,
To hold us in his realm imprisoned.
Halleluja!

BACH: CHORUS FROM CANTATA NO. 71, *GOTT IST MEIN KÖNIG* (p. 167)

Dein Alter sei wie deine Jugend

Thy later years shall be like thy youth,
and God is with thee in everything that thou dost.

Unit III

BRUMEL: "SUB DIVERSIS SPECIEBUS" FROM *LAUDA, SION, SALVATOREM* (p. 188)

Lo! beneath what appears dual
(But is a sign only), is hidden a jewel
Far beyond creation's reach.

ISAAC: TRACT FROM *CHORALIS CONSTANTINUS* (p. 191)

Ave Maria

Hail Mary, full of grace, the Lord is with thee.

LASSUS: *OCULUS NON VIDIT* (p. 192)

Eye hath not seen, nor ear heard,
Neither have entered into the heart of man,
The things which God hath prepared for them
That love Him.

LASSUS: *JUSTUS COR SUUM TRADET* (p. 193)

The just man will give his heart early
To the Lord who hath made him, and he will pray
In the sight of the most High.

LASSUS: *QUI SEQUITUR ME* (p. 195)

He that followeth me shall not walk in darkness
But shall have the light of life (said the Lord).

FESTA: *AMOR CHE MI CONSIGLI?* (p. 197)

Love, how shall I counsel myself?
I wish to flee her yet to follow her . . .
You know that to have peace or even a truce from her
I never hope; then it would be better to flee
before I am entirely consumed,
since following her would ever slay me;
If she is silent, speaks or laughs
it is serious cause of the greatest pain and death;
alas! pitiless fate!
how it has placed me in such a perilous plight!
Love, do I not know how to counsel myself?

Unit IV

LASSUS: MOTET, *LAUDABO NOMEN DEI* (p. 210)

Praise the name of God with song,
and extol him in hymns of praise.

PALESTRINA: "PARS MEA DOMINUS" FROM *LAMENTATIONS* (p. 212)

The Lord is my portion, said my soul:
therefore, will I wait for him.

VICTORIA: MOTET, *O MAGNUM MYSTERIUM* (p. 220)

O mighty mystery,
and awesome sacrament,
as animals see the Lord born,
while lying in the manger.
O blessed Virgin,
whose womb was worthy
to bear the Lord Jesus Christ.
Halleluia.

JOSQUIN: *MILLE REGRETZ* (p. 227)

Thousand regrets to leave you and be far away from your loving face,
My sorrow and pain are so great,
That my days will be seen to come to an end.

ARCADELT: *IO MI RIVOLGO INDIETRO* (p. 230)

I look back at every step
With a body weary of bearing great pain.
And then take comfort from your atmosphere,
Which makes me turn forward, saying: alas!
Then thinking again of the sweet delight I leave,
Of the long road and my brief life,
I end my plaint dismayed and wan,
And cast down my weeping eyes to earth.

MONTEVERDI: MADRIGAL, *SE NEL PARTIR DA VOI* (p. 234)

If I left you, my life would be so gravely tormented.
Oh! rather than think of ever leaving, my Lady, I would die.

And since on leaving you I feel such misery
I would first die than ever leave.

GESUALDO: MADRIGAL, *RESTA DI DARMI NOIA* (p. 239)

Cease to give me anguish,
Cruel and false thought,
That I can never be the one who pleases you!
Death is joy for me,
Wherein hope is forbidden,
Thus to be happy nevermore.

Unit V

COMPOSITE ORGANUM AT THE FIFTH (*MUSICA ENCHIRIADIS*) (p. 255)

Sit gloria Domini

Glory be to the Lord, in eternity will the Lord rejoice in his works.

12th CENTURY: *MIRA LEGE, MIRO MODO* (p. 256)

Wondrous law, wondrous way, God forms man.
Yet more wondrous He reforms him.
See the wondrous order!

MELISMATIC ORGANUM: *CUNCTIPOTENS GENITOR* (p. 257)

All-powerful Father, God, Creator of all, have mercy upon us.
Christ, form of God, virtue and wisdom of the Father, have mercy upon us.
Sacred spirit of both, united love, have mercy upon us.

HYMN IN CONDUCTUS STYLE: *NATO NOBIS HODIE* (p. 258)

Born to us on this day
of the Virgin Mary
eternal ruler in glory.
With sweet jubilation
we give thanks to God.

13th CENTURY: MOTET, *O MITISSIMA (QUANT VOI)—VIRGO—HEC DIES* (p. 259)

Quant voi

When I see returning the season of summer, that the woods resound with the little birds,
then I weep and sigh because of the great desire which I feel for the fair Marion,
who has imprisoned my heart.

O mitissima

O sweetest Virgin Mary, implore thy Son to give us help and remedy
against the deceiving tricks of the demons and their iniquities.

Virgo

Virgin of virgins, light of lights, reformer of men, who bore the Lord,
through thee, O Mary, let grace come, as the angel announced,
thou who art virgin before and after.

Hec dies

This is the day (which the Lord hath made).

MAGISTER PIERO: CACCIA, *SEGUGI A CORDE* (p. 263)

I followed the chords and dogs through the forest.
Up and down, here and there, with a
"Woof, woof, woof, woof!"
And the hunters calling and assuring,
"Look there, look there, look!"
"Dragon, dragon, to you, to you!"
"Olla, olla, olla!" "What is it, what is it,
Come here, come here, for here are the bears!"
So said one as he ran to the hunt,
While to another hunt I raced.

     Ritornello: A little way from the woods.

At the sound of the horns and the other tumult,
From a valley came the country lass.
"Ai, ai, ai, there, there, after the fox!"
Then I took her by the hand, "Come here, Here let the fox go!"
She said, "Oh no, oh no, since I don't want to!"
Yet pride was of no avail as I embraced her;
And led her into the woods.

Unit VI

BRAHMS: CHORALE PRELUDE, *O WIE SELIG SEID IHR DOCH* (p. 293)

Oh how blessed are ye pious ones,
Who through death have come to God.
You have escaped all misery,
Which still holds us imprisoned.

Unit VII

STRAVINSKY: *SYMPHONY OF PSALMS* (p. 307)

    Psalm 39, Verses 2 and 3

With expectation I have waited for the Lord,
    and He was attentive to me.
And He heard my prayers, and brought me out of the pit of misery
    and the mire of dregs.

DATES OF COMPOSERS

Arcadelt, Jacob (c. 1505-c. 1560)
Bach, Johann Christian (1735-1782)
Bach, Johann Sebastian (1685-1750)
Bartók, Béla (1881-1945)
Beethoven, Ludwig van (1770-1827)
Brahms, Johannes (1833-1897)
Brumel, Antoine (c. 1475-c. 1520)
Buxtehude, Dietrich (c. 1637-1707)
Byrd, William (1543-1623)
Cavazzoni, Marco Antonio da Bologna
    (c. 1490-c. 1570)
Corelli, Arcangelo (1653-1713)
Des Prez, Josquin (c. 1445-1521)
Dufay, Guillaume (c. 1400-1474)
Festa, Costanzo (c. 1490-1545)
Fischer, Johann Kaspar Ferdinand
    (c. 1665-1746)
Frescobaldi, Girolamo (1583-1643)
Froberger, Johann Jakob (1616-1667)
Gesualdo, Don Carlo (c. 1560-1613)
Handel, Georg Friedrich (1685-1759)
Harris, Roy (1898-   )
Hindemith, Paul (1895-1963)
Isaac, Heinrich (c. 1450-1517)

Lassus, Roland de (1532-1594)
Machaut, Guillaume de (c. 1300-1377)
Monteverdi, Claudio (1567-1643)
Morley, Thomas (1557-1602)
Mozart, Wolfgang Amadeus (1756-1791)
Obrecht, Jacob (1452-1505)
Ockeghem, Johannes (1430-1495)
Pachelbel, Johann (1653-1706)
Palestrina, Giovanni Pierluigi
    (c. 1525-1594)
Piero, Magister (14th century)
Purcell, Henry (c. 1659-1695)
Rameau, Jean-Philippe (1685-1764)
Reger, Max (1873-1916)
Scarlatti, Domenico (1685-1757)
Scheidt, Samuel (1587-1654)
Schütz, Heinrich (1585-1672)
Stravinsky, Igor (1882-   )
Sweelinck, Jan Pieterszoon
    (1562-1621)
Tomkins, Thomas (1572-1656)
Victoria, Tomás Luis de (1549-1611)
Vivaldi, Antonio (c. 1678-1741)
Webern, Anton von (1883-1945)